art / shop / eat
PRAGUE

Jasper Tilbury

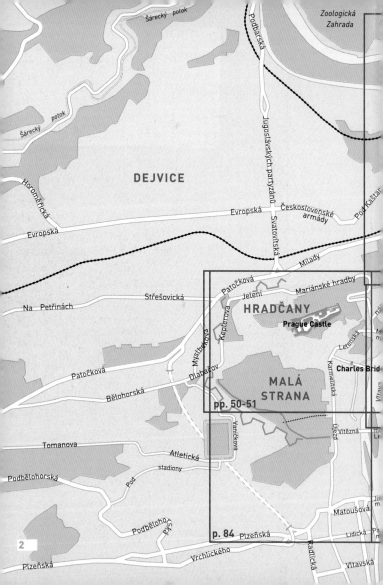

Zoologická Zahrada

Šárecký potok

Podbabská

Šárecký potok

Horoměřická

DEJVICE

Jugoslávských partyzánů

Evropská

Svatovítská

Československé armády

Pod Kaštar

Evropská

Milady

Na Petřinách

Střešovická

Patočková

Jelení

Mariánské hradby

Keplerova

HRADČANY

Prague Castle

Mysbehova

Lerenská

Patočková

Dlabačov

Karmelitská

Charles Brid

Bělohorská

MALÁ STRANA

Vlta

Tomanova

Atletická

stadiony

Pod

Vaníčkova

Újezd Vítězná

Podbělohorská

Podbělohor ska

p. 84 Plzeňská

Matoušová

Lidická

Plzeňská

Vrchlického

Radlická

Vltavská

pp. 50–51

2

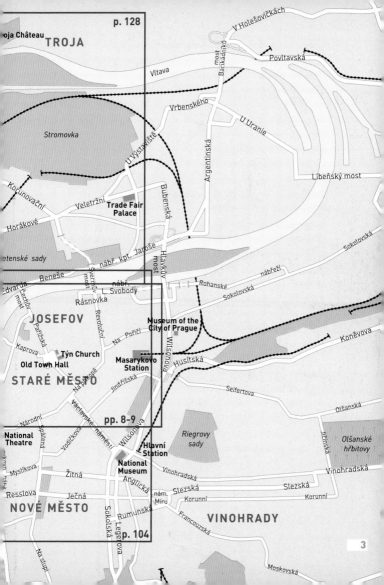

The Old Town & Jewish Quarter

Prague Castle & the Hradčany

The Little Quarter (Malá Strana)

The New Town (Nové Město)

The Trade Fair Palace & Troja Château

entertainment

planning

art glossary

index

introduction

'Magical Prague'—the term is almost a cliché, yet this is the city where the emperor Rudolf II immersed himself in alchemy and the occult, where Doctor Faustus sold his soul to the devil, and where Rabbi Löw fashioned his golem from the mud of the Vltava. Writers, Kafka and Kisch among them, have found inspiration in Prague's haunting, almost disturbing quality. Casting his gaze over the red rooftops and Gothic spires from the top of Petřín Hill, Milan Kundera was even moved to call it 'the most beautiful city in the world'.

Few cities of comparable size can boast a cultural complexity as rich as Prague's. The wealth of medieval and Renaissance monuments is astonishing, even obscuring the city's huge contribution to the Baroque and Rococo. It was here, too, that Mucha's Art Nouveau exuberance reigned; where Mozart premiered Don Giovanni, dedicating it to the 'good people of Prague'; and where the beauty and originality of Czech Functionalist architecture found expression in the Trade Fair Palace, today the city's best modern art gallery.

In the fifteen years since the fall of Communism, Prague has been developing at breakneck speed. The modern city is hardly comparable to the Prague of old. Widespread restoration has injected new life into ancient monuments, and ambitious new buildings are being designed by a generation of architects too young to remember Communism.

A vastly improved restaurant scene has enhanced Prague's appeal as a tourist destination. In addition to traditional Czech fare, you'll find French, Thai, Indian and Japanese cuisine. Strictly speaking, Prague is not a shopping city, with largely unremarkable souvenir shops filling the main tourist areas. But off the beaten track, visitors can discover treasures hidden in the city's charming side streets. Antique shops are filled with garnet jewellery, silverware and objets d'art, while the famous Bohemian crystal is available everywhere in traditional and contemporary designs. Handmade textiles, ceramics and wooden toys are also sold all over Prague.

THE OLD TOWN &
JEWISH QUARTER

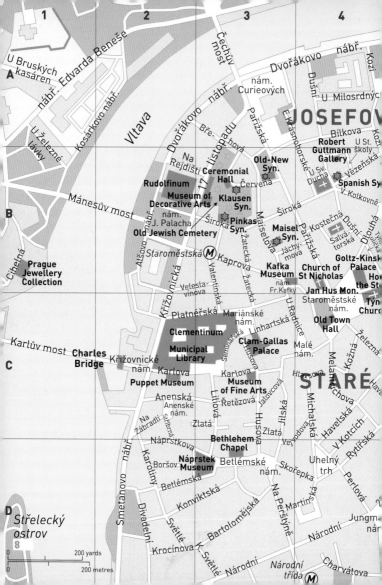

1 **2** **3** **4**

A

U Bruských kasáren

nábř. Edvarda Beneše

Kosárkovo nábř.

U Železné lávky

Vltava

Čechův most

Dvořákovo nábř.

nám. Curieových

JOSEFOV

Dušní

U Milosrdnýc

Kozí

Dvořákovo nábř.

Pařížská

Bílkova

Robert Guttmann Gallery

U St. školy

Věženská

Elišky Krásnohorské

B

Mánesův most

Na Rejdišti

17. listopadu

Břehová

Rudolfinum

Museum of Decorative Arts

nám. J. Palacha

Ceremonial Hall

Červená

Klausen Syn.

Pinkas Syn.

Široká

Maiselova

Old-New Syn.

Maisel Syn.

U Sv. Ducha

Spanish Sy

V. Kolkovně

Pařížská

Kostečná

Dušní

Dlouhá

Old Jewish Cemetery

Široká

Žatecká

Staroměstská Ⓜ Kaprova

Jáchymova

Salvá-torská

Cihelná

Prague Jewellery Collection

Alšovo nábř.

Křížovnická

Valentinská

Žatecká

Veleslavínova

Kafka Museum

nám. Fr. Kafky

U Radnice

Church of St Nicholas

Jan Hus Mon.

Staroměstské nám.

Goltz-Kinsk Palace

Ho the St

Týn Churc

C

Karlův most

Charles Bridge

Křížovnické nám.

Platnéřská

Clementinum

Municipal Library

Mariánské nám.

Linhartská

Seminářská

Clam-Gallas Palace

Malé nám.

Old Town Hall

Hlavova

Melantri

Kožná

Železná

STARÉ

Karlova

Puppet Museum

Anenská

Anenské nám.

Na Zábradlí

Stříbrná

Liliová

Zlatá

Karlova

Museum of Fine Arts

Řetězová

Jalovcová

Husova

Jilská

Vejvodova

Michalská

Havelská

V Kotcích

Uhelný trh

Rytířská

Perlova

Náprstkova

Boršov

Bethlehem Chapel

Zlatá

Betlémské nám.

Skořepka

Na Perštýně

Martinská

Náprstek Museum

Betlémská

Karoliny

Konviktská

Bartolomějská

Martins

Jungm nár

D

Smetanovo nábř.

Divadelní

Světlá

K. Světlé

Krocínova

Národní

Národní třída Ⓜ

Charvátova

Střelecký ostrov

8

200 yards

200 metres

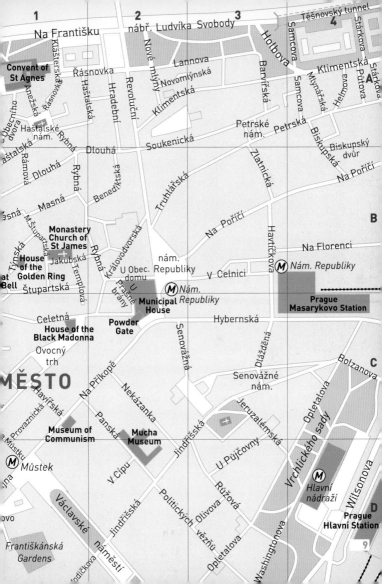

Prague's Old Town

The medieval urban plan of the Old Town (or Staré Město), with its web of narrow streets fanning out from Old Town Square, adds picturesque charm to a city already steeped in the picturesque. Within this small geographical area lies a treasure trove of historic monuments, churches, palaces and museums. It is, however, the tourist heart of Prague, and in summer the sheer volume and noise of human traffic can be oppressive. Visitors to the Old Town are inevitably drawn to its lively hub: the beautiful Old Town Square (Staroměstské náměstí), an architectural showpiece unrivalled in Central Europe. A cluster of cafés in the south-west corner of the square provides an excellent vantage point from which to admire the square's most celebrated landmarks, including Old Town Hall's famous Astronomical Clock.

Old Town Hall

OPEN	April–Oct: Mon, 11 am–6 pm; Tues–Sun, 9 am–6 pm Nov–March: Mon, 11 am–5 pm; Tues–Sun, 9 am–5 pm
CHARGES	40 Kč interior; 30 Kč tower
TELEPHONE	236 002 562 (tours and information)
MAIN ENTRANCE	Staroměstské náměstí 1
METRO	Staroměstská
DISABLED ACCESS	The lift to the top of the tower is designed for wheelchair access.
GUIDED VISITS	The interiors can only be seen with a guided tour, arranged through the on-site PIS info centre They take place at irregular intervals throughout the day.
SHOP	Guides, books and souvenirs are sold in the foyer.
EAT	There are plenty of cafés and restaurants around the square.

HIGHLIGHTS
Astronomical Clock
'At the Minute' House
Town Hall Tower

The heavily restored Old Town Hall (Staroměstská radnice), which projects into the south-west corner of Old Town Square, is the square's principal tourist attraction. Its history is a complex one; it's really several buildings, the earliest of which dates back to the beginning of the 14th C. Most impressive is the 70m-high tower, built in 1364. This is where the large crowds gather every hour on the hour to watch the chiming of the famous Astronomical Clock (see next page). The north wing of the Old Town Hall was burnt down by the Nazis on the penultimate day of World War II; there were plans to put up a modern extension on the site, but they seem to have been abandoned.

EXTERIOR
A **chapel**, with a delightful oriel window projecting east, was added to the first floor of the tower in 1381; the wall beneath the oriel has a plaque bearing the names of 27 Protestant leaders

11

Apostles, ready to take their turn as the Astronomical Clock strikes

beheaded here in 1621 for participating in the Battle of the White Mountain (the exact place of the execution is marked by white crosses on the paving stones nearby). The battle is considered to be the first clash of the Thirty Years' War, and saw Bohemian Protestants routed by Austrian Imperial and Catholic forces.

To the west of the **Astronomical Clock** extends a row of houses bought up by the civic authorities over the centuries and gradually incorporated into the Town Hall. These include the former Kříž House, purchased in 1360, which features an attractive Renaissance window with the Latin inscription *Praga caput regni* ('Prague, capital of the kingdom'). The finest property, known as **'At the Minute' (Dům U minuty)**, is situated at the very end. It's where the Kafka family lived from 1889 right up to the time of its purchase in 1896. The exterior of the house is covered with *sgraffiti* that are among the finest in Prague, representing Classical and Biblical scenes and allegorical figures of the Virtues. They were made c. 1611 and restored in 1919 by the Cubist painter Josef Čapek (they were restored again after 1945).

THE ASTRONOMICAL CLOCK

Installed originally by the master clocksmith Mikoláš of Kadaň in 1410, the clock was rebuilt in 1490 by a teacher at the Charles University, Master Hanuš of Růže. According to legend, Hanuš was blinded to prevent him from creating another such marvel, and in retaliation, he climbed up the tower and stopped the clock. The true story is that the clock's mechanism was not perfected until 1560, after which it required no further alterations. Only its decorations changed—the painted calendar on the lower level is an 1865 copy by Josef Mánes (the original is kept in the Museum of the City of Prague). The middle level is the clock proper, which tells the time according to three conventions (Central European, Old Bohemian, Babylonian) and gives the position of the sun and moon in relation to the signs of the Zodiac, from which one can ascertain the date.

At the striking of each hour an impressive spectacle begins, with a figure of Death raising an hourglass and pulling a funerary bell. Windows open on the upper level and a procession of Apostles files past, bowing to onlookers. At the corners of the clock are three more allegorical figures perched on pinnacles—Vanity, an Ottoman Turk and Greed (represented by a Jew gloating over his sack of gold)—reflecting the anxieties of the medieval mind. Below these are a further four figures representing Astronomy, History, Philosophy and Religion.

INTERIOR

Though it has been much altered over the centuries and was badly gutted in 1945, the first floor of the Town Hall still has a late-Gothic **Council Chamber** of 1470 and an adjoining chapel (reconstructed) designed by Petr Parléř in 1381 (it still has remnants of medieval frescoes and an oriel window). The Gothic vaulting in the **vestibule** of the building has a mosaic decoration of 1937, designed by Mikoláš Aleš, representing the legend of the mythical Princess Libuše. Libuše was a 9th-C ruler and prophet who, after being criticised for her celibacy, decided to take a husband (in a suitably mysterious way). She sent her henchmen into the forest with orders to found a town at the spot where they

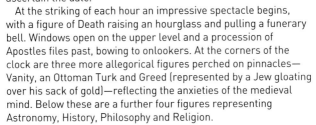

Monument to Jan Hus

saw a ploughman (*Přemysl*) building the threshold (*práh*) of a house. Libuše married him (so establishing the Přemyslid dynasty), founding the town that became Praha, or Prague.

From the vestibule, stairs lead down to the recently opened **dungeon**, which has evidence of fire damage from World War II when the building was used by the Czechoslovak Resistance.

The highlight of a visit to the Town Hall is the excellent **view** from the viewing gallery at the top of the tower.

MONUMENT TO JAN HUS

This extraordinary bronze monument sits near the centre of the Old Town Square and indeed dominates the space. It is the masterpiece of idiosyncratic sculptor Ladislav Šaloun, who began planning the work as early as 1898 and struggled with it for the next 17 years. Considered by some to be completely out of place in the square, it is nonetheless one of the most powerful public monuments in any European city, and one which brilliantly complements its surroundings.

It commemorates the religious reformer Jan Hus (1373–1415),

who was burnt at the stake at Constance in 1415 for speaking out against the corruption of the Church and propagating what his inquisitors saw as heretical teachings. The monument, which bears at its base the preacher's words, 'The truth will prevail', features the figure of Hus rising above a struggling sea of gesticulating people, in a defiant posture reminiscent of one of Rodin's *Burghers of Calais*; the power of this detailed yet unified composition lies to a large extent in the way in which—even on the brightest of days—it forms a dark and menacing profile against the light and cheerful background of the square, vividly reminding the spectator of the bleaker moments in Czech history.

The unveiling of the monument was scheduled for 1915—the 500th anniversary of Hus's death—but few worse moments could have been chosen for the completion of a highly emotive monument symbolising the fight for Czech independence. The unveiling went ahead as planned, but the Austrian authorities did not permit a ceremony. In response, locals completely covered the monument with flowers, and within a few days all that showed of it was a solitary finger pointing menacingly to the sky. The continuing symbolic power of the monument was attested in the wake of the Soviet invasion of August 1968, when it was shrouded in black drapes.

Church of Our Lady Before Týn

OPEN	Access extremely limited, can only be guaranteed during services (currently Sat 8 am and Sun 11 am, but changes frequently).
CHARGES	Free admission
MAIN ENTRANCE	Staroměstské náměstí (enter through No. 14)
METRO	Staroměstská
DISABLED ACCESS	Yes

The Týn Church

HIGHLIGHTS
14th-C north portal
16th-C *Baptism of Christ*
17th-C tombstone of Tycho Brahe
17th-C high altar

This church (Matky boží pred Týnem), which looms at the eastern
end of the Old Town Square, is the most prominent building in
the Old Town. Work on the present structure began in 1365, and
in the early 15th C the place became the main church of the
Hussites in Prague, and would remain associated with the
followers of Jan Hus until 1621—the Hussite monarch George of
Poděbrady would become one of the church's greatest
benefactors. Under his reign the west façade's tall gable and the
northern tower were erected. The gable was adorned with a
statue of George and a gold chalice symbolising the Hussite
cause, but these were removed after the Battle of the White
Mountain and replaced with an image of the Virgin (her halo was
made from the gold of the chalice).

As with most medieval churches in Bohemia, the gloomy pile of
exposed masonry that is the twin-towered exterior does not rise
directly from the square, but is set back behind a row of arcaded
houses, in this case a house of Romanesque origin with a tall late-
18th-C façade (No. 15, at the south-east end of the square), and
the attractive Týn School (No. 14), which has a pair of stepped
16th-C gables recalling those of the Scuola Grande di San Marco
in Venice.

   The north portal, adorned with a fine copy of a late-14th C
tympanum of the Crucifixion from the workshop of Petr Parléř, is
reached along the narrow Týnská, which runs along the northern
side of the Týn School. Off this path is a gateway (just to the east
of the church) leading into the merchants' courtyard (Týn) which
gave this area its name (the courtyard is also known by its
German name of Ungelt).

   The Týn church is a three-aisled hall with unadorned plaster
from the Baroque period. At the western end of the north aisle is
a fine **Gothic baldachin** (1493), but the outstanding work of art in

the building is the intricately carved *Baptism of Christ* by the
Monogramist I.P. (c. 1526), on the pier immediately to the right of
the south portal. Attached to the south-aisle pier directly in front
of the main apse is the red marble tombstone of the Danish
astronomer **Tycho Brahe**, who died in 1601. Legend has it he died
as a result of trying to hold back his urine while in the presence of
Emperor Rudolph II ('I don't want to die like Tycho Brahe' is the
Czech expression for 'I'm desperate for a pee'), but subsequent
research has found that his death was caused by mercury
poisoning. Nobody knows whether it was an accidental overdose—
in those days mercury was used medicinally—or murder.

Charles Bridge

OPEN	Always open
CHARGES	Free
MAIN ENTRANCE	Karlův most (closed to traffic)
METRO	Staroměstská or Malostranská
DISABLED ACCESS	Yes
EAT	There are cafés and restaurants on the beautiful Kampa Island

HIGHLIGHTS

17th-C *St John of Nepomuk*
18th-C *Vision of St Luitgard*
18th-C *Sts John of Matha, Felix de Valois and Ivo*

The Charles Bridge (Karlův most), one of Europe's most beautiful
bridges, is not simply the visual centrepiece of Prague, but has
also played a central role in the city's life and history. Despite the
now almost oppressive congestion of pedestrians, souvenir stalls
and street bands, it is hard not to feel an acute sense of drama

and expectation when you first see the statuary and the Little Quarter's turreted entrance gate, behind which rises the massive dome of St Nicholas and, higher still, the dramatic silhouette of Prague Castle. Indeed, the views on all sides on the bridge are uninterruptedly beautiful. The place becomes especially evocative on a winter's night when, in the dim light of lanterns, a freezing mist rises from the river, and isolated groups of pedestrians glide past and disappear into the gloom.

Commissioned in the late 14th C by the Emperor Charles IV, the bridge was a remarkable feat of medieval engineering, designed by the brilliant architect, Petr Parléř. The 16-arch structure, a full 500 metres in length, links the Old Town with the Little Quarter. For centuries it was Prague's only bridge spanning the Vltava. Built of massive sandstone blocks, and guarded at either end by picturesque medieval gates and towers, the bridge has been damaged on several occasions by floods but has never collapsed.

As well as serving as part of the processional route of the Bohemian kings, the Charles Bridge was a place where commerce took place, tournaments were held, customs duties collected, lawsuits settled, criminals executed, and delinquents punished by being dipped in the Vltava in wicker baskets. The most famous incident in its history occurred on March 20, 1393, when the future St John of Nepomuk—an obscure prelate who had fallen afoul of Wenceslas IV—was bound hand and foot and thrown from its parapet into the river. According to legend, his body floated on the water for an unnaturally long time, a constellation of stars hovering above it. In 1683, at a time when the Jesuits were beginning to promote the Nepomuk cult, a statue of him was placed on the bridge, near the supposed point from where he was flung. This led to several religious orders commissioning other Baroque statues for the bridge, which were all in place by 1714. From the mid-19th C onwards several other statues were added, and some of the more worn ones were replaced by copies.

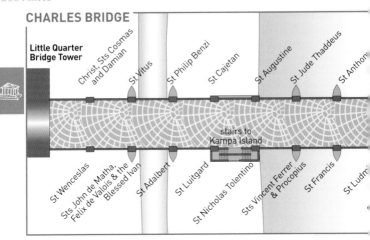

CHARLES BRIDGE

Little Quarter
Bridge Tower

Christ, Sts Cosmas and Damian

St Vitus

St Philip Benzi

St Cajetan

St Augustine

St Jude Thaddeus

St Anthon'

stairs to
Kampa Island

St Wenceslas

Sts John de Matha,
Felix de Valois & the
Blessed Ivan

St Adalbert

St Luitgard

St Nicholas Tolentino

Sts Vincent Ferrer
& Procopius

St Francis

St Ludm'

THE STATUES

With its gallery of 30 statues (most now copies), the Charles Bridge is a veritable museum of Bohemian sculpture. On the first pier to the right (walking east to west) stands *Madonna and St Bernard* (1709) by **Matěj Jäckel**, a sculptor who introduced to Bohemia the dynamic high-flown style of the Italian artist Bernini. This style was used to extremely expressive effect in the work of **Matthias Braun**, an Austrian-born sculptor who first came to Bohemia in 1710 to execute statues for the Charles Bridge; a copy of the second statue that he did here, representing *St Ivo* (1711), the patron saint of lawyers, can be seen on the left-hand side, directly opposite Jäckel's Madonna. The other outstanding Bohemian sculptor of this period was **Ferdinand Brokoff**, who carried out several works for the bridge, including the sculptural group of *Sts Barbara, Margaret and Elizabeth* that adorns the second pier on the left-hand side.

The first monument to be placed on the bridge was a gilded bronze crucifix, which was set up on the third pier to the right in 1657; the two stone figures were executed by **Emmanuel Max** in 1861, while the Hebrew inscription on the cross ('Holy Holy Holy is

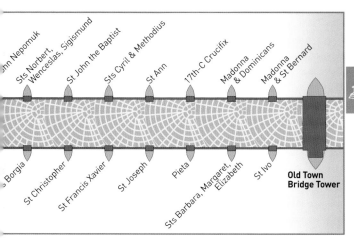

Labels on the diagram (top, left to right): John Nepomuk; Sts Norbert, Wenceslas, Sigismund; St John the Baptist; Sts Cyril & Methodius; St Ann; 17th-C Crucifix; Madonna & Dominicans; Madonna & St Bernard

Labels on the diagram (bottom, left to right): s Borgia; St Christopher; St Francis Xavier; St Joseph; Pieta; Sts Barbara, Margaret, Elizabeth; St Ivo; **Old Town Bridge Tower**

Our Lord'), dating from 1696, is said to have been paid for by a Jew as a fine for mocking this Christian symbol.

Between the sixth and seventh piers on the right is a small cross marking the supposed spot where St John of Nepomuk was thrown into the Vltava in 1393; the bronze statue of the saint, with a gold-leaf halo, stands on the eighth pier to the right, and was executed by **Jan Brokoff** in the 1680s. The relief at the base of the statue depicts a weathered scene of St John's martyrdom, which is said to bring good luck if you touch it.

Towards its western end the bridge crosses the picturesque **Kampa Island** (see p. 95), sometimes referred to as the 'Venice of Prague'. Above the steps leading down to it, on the twelfth pier to the left, is a sculpture of *The Vision of St Luitgard* (1710), the first work that Matthias Braun made in Prague, and in many ways the most powerful and emotionally compelling on the bridge. Tradition has it that the work was based on a design by Petr Brandl, and there is certainly something very painterly in its wildly agitated drapery.

Two piers further along to the left is another sculptural masterpiece: a group by Ferdinand Brokoff featuring *Sts John of*

Matha, Felix de Valois and Ivo, with a Turk guarding a group of captured Christians (1714). The whole is carved with Brokoff's characteristic realism (note, in particular, the face of the Turk); the work was commissioned as a gesture of thanks to the Trinitarian Order for having redeemed Christians from Turkish captivity. Directly opposite this group is Brokoff's *St Vitus* (1714), the only marble work on the bridge (the other stone sculptures are made of sandstone).

Convent of St Agnes

OPEN	Open Tues–Sun, 10 am–6 pm
CHARGES	100/50 Kč; 150 Kč families; free on public holidays
TELEPHONE	224 810 628. For general information about the National Gallery's exhibitions: 222 321 459
WEB	www.ngprague.cz
MAIN ENTRANCE	U Milosrdných 17
METRO	náměstí Republiky or Staroměstská
DISABLED ACCESS	Yes. Ask at reception if you are interested in the special exhibition with braille captions.
GUIDED VISITS	Tours in English or French organised by the National Gallery's education departments; 1200 Kč for groups up to 15 persons; 1500 Kč for groups over 15 persons; plus standard admission fee. Bookings: 221 87 92 16
SHOP	Gallery shop sells books and catalogues.
EAT	There are plenty of cafés and restaurants in the area to the south and west.

HIGHLIGHTS
14th-C *Vyšší Brod Altarpiece*
14th-C portraits of saints by Master Theodoric
14th-C *Třeboň Altarpiece*
16th-C *Lamentation of Christ* **from Žebrák**

The Třeboň Altarpiece

The Convent of St Agnes (Klášter sv. Anežky české) is a large and important medieval complex sometimes pompously referred to as the 'Bohemian Assisi'. It was founded for the Poor Clares by Wenceslas I in 1233, probably on the request of his sister, Agnes of Bohemia (1211–1292), who would become the first abbess, as well as a patron saint of Bohemia when she was canonised in 1989 by Pope John Paul II. Emperor Joseph II dissolved the convent for good in 1782, after which the buildings fell into decay and were used as workshops. Extensive restoration work was begun in the 20th C, during which foundations of a neighbouring Franciscan monastery of the early 13th C were discovered. The convent now houses the National Gallery's collection of medieval Bohemian and Central European art, with altarpieces, painting and sculpture.

THE BUILDING

The museum in the convent is centred around a cloister that has largely retained its mid-13th-C appearance, apart from the upper level of the eastern side, which features a **Renaissance arcade** built by the Dominicans. At the cloister's southeast corner is a door leading into the convent's **two adjoining churches**. The earlier of the two was dedicated to St Francis and completed by the mid-13th C; however, only its presbytery has survived. Today it is used for concerts. Projecting east of this structure is the spacious and elegant **Sanctuary of St Saviour**, which dates from the 1280s, and is a fine example of French Gothic influence; it is also the resting place of St Agnes.

THE MUSEUM - MEDIEVAL ART IN BOHEMIA AND CENTRAL EUROPE

The first major Bohemian painter represented in the museum is the anonymous **Master of the Vyšší Brod Altarpiece** *(ROOM 2)*. This altarpiece of c. 1350, from a former Cistercian monastery in Southern Bohemia, comprises nine panels of scenes from the life of Christ and the Virgin. The work of the Master of Vyšší Brod, like that of many other Bohemian artists of the period, is permeated

CONVENT OF ST AGNES

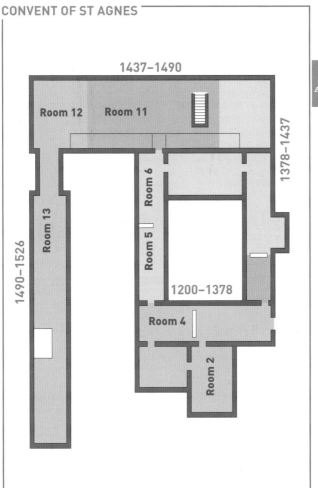

with Italian—in particular, Sienese—influence. This can largely be attributed to the Emperor Charles IV (1346–78), who summoned new monastic orders and Italian artists to Prague as part of his lifelong effort to turn the city into 'the second Rome'. The most idiosyncratic painter in Charles's circle, and one of the earliest Bohemian artists known by name, was **Master Theodoric** *(ROOM 3)*, who is best known for the panels and murals he painted at Karlštejn Castle near Prague in 1357–65. He is represented here by six large and luminously modelled heads of saints and Church fathers.

A work of great historical interest is the *Votive Panel of Jan Očko of Vlašim* (before 1371) in *ROOM 4*. It portrays the enthroned Madonna flanked by what are sometimes considered to be the earliest examples of Bohemian portraiture—remarkably realistic representations of Charles IV, Wenceslas IV and the panel's donor, Jan Očko, the Archbishop of Prague. In contrast to earlier altarpieces, in which each figure occupied a one panel of a polyptych, this work recalls an Italian *sacra conversazione*: the figures are aware of each other and appear in a unified space.

The reign of Charles's successor Wenceslas IV (1378–1419) coincided with Bohemian art's Golden Age, when International Gothic came to the fore in both painting and sculpture. This style rejected the naturalism characteristic of the work of Master Theodoric in favour of a return to the sensual and the ideal, espousing soft and gentle rhythms, especially in the flow of drapery. Its chief exponent in Bohemia was the anonymous **Master of the Třeboň Altarpiece** *(ROOM 5)*, whose art had strong affinities with contemporary Burgundian artists such as Melchior Broederlam. His principal work (see picture on p. 23), from which he derives his name, was painted c. 1390 for the former Augustinian church of St Giles in the southern Bohemian town of Třeboň. Unfortunately, only three of its panels, painted on both sides with vivid colours and charming detail, have survived.

Several fine votive panels were produced in the wake of the Třeboň Altarpiece, most notably the *Epitaph of Jan of Jeřeň* (1395), a canon at Vitus's Cathedral in Prague. The painting, in *ROOM 6*, shows the Virgin with the infant Christ standing on her knees and, to the right, strikingly colourful figures of Sts Bartholomew and Thomas.

In the mid-15th C, Bohemia's links with European art were severed as a consequence of the Hussite Wars. They were not revived until the 1470s, when Nuremberg, and later Cologne, became the new centres of influence. Attention to detail and the three-dimensionality of picture planes—hallmarks of the Netherlandish style of Rogier van der Weyden and Dieric Bouts—entered Bohemian art via Cologne. They feature in the anonymous *Altarpiece of the Master of the Knights of the Cross, Mikuláš Puchner* (1482), which deals with the legend of Agnes of Bohemia; one panel shows the eponymous heroine—to whom the convent is dedicated—tending to the sick in a scene of astonishing realism *(ROOM 11)*.

An example of masterly draughtsmanship is provided by **Albrecht Dürer**'s exquisite series of 15 woodcuts known as the *Apocalypse* (1498) in *ROOM 12* . This was the first book to be entirely illustrated, printed and published by a single artist. The work, featuring a fantastical multi-headed beast, bears all the characteristic traits of Dürer's vivid, expressive and iconographic style.

The last of the outstanding Bohemian painters represented at the museum is the **Master of the Litoměřice Altarpiece**, who is sometimes identified with the German artist **Hans Elfelder**; he was at any rate someone who had been brought up in South Germany and might also have had first-hand knowledge of North Italian art. The altarpiece from which he derives his name is currently in the North Bohemian Gallery at Litoměřice, but there are a number of other impressive works associated with him here, most notably a series of panels from the Týn church (c. 1510) showing Sts Barbara and Catherine, and a triptych of *The Holy Trinity* (1515–20).

Of the later sculptures, special mention should be made of the expressive early 16th-C relief of the *Lamentation of Christ* from Žebrák in *ROOM 13* by the artist known as the **Monogramist I.P.**, who seems to have come from the Passau or Salzburg region. This artist was also responsible for the *Votive Altarpiece from Zlíchov*—a series of eight intricately carved reliefs, including a superb central one of Christ the Saviour.

The Jewish Quarter

OLD-NEW SYNAGOGUE
OLD JEWISH CEMETERY
KLAUSEN SYNAGOGUE
MAISEL SYNAGOGUE
PINKAS SYNAGOGUE
SPANISH SYNAGOGUE
THE ROBERT GUTTMANN GALLERY

OPEN
All the sites of the Jewish Museum are open Nov–Mar,
9 am–4.30 pm; and Apr–Oct, 9 am–6 pm.
The Old-New Synagogue is open Nov–Mar, Sun–Thur,
9 am–4.30 pm; Fri, 9 am–2 pm; and Apr–Oct, Sun–Thur,
9 am–6 pm; Fri, 9 am–5 pm.

CLOSED
Sat; Jewish holidays

CHARGES
Jewish Museum 300/250 Kč;under 6 years free. Tickets can be
bought from the Reservation Centre at U Starého hřbitova 3a
or from any of the ticket offices in the surrounding area (male
visitors are provided with skullcaps). A **single ticket** covers
entry to the Old Jewish Cemetery (see below), Maisel
Synagogue, Klausen Synagogue, Pinkas Synagogue, Spanish
Synagogue and Robert Guttman Gallery. Tickets to the **Old-
New Synagogue** (200/140 Kč), which is not part of the Jewish
Museum, can be bought from the ticket office/gift shop at
Červená 4; the ticket also covers entry to the Jubilee
Synagogue, outside the area of the former ghetto.

TELEPHONE
222 317 191 (Jewish Museum); 222 319 002 (Jewish
Community of Prague)

WEB
www.jewishmuseum.cz

MAIN ENTRANCE
Old-New Synagogue Červená 2
Old Jewish Cemetery Entrance is usually on U Starého
hřbitova, but since the floods of 2002 it has been moved to
Široká 3, with the old entrance now the exit. This situation is
expected to remain until renovation work on the Pinkas
Synagogue is complete.
Maisel Synagogue Maiselova 10
Klausen Synagogue U Starého hřbitova 3a
Pinkas Synagogue Široká 3
Spanish Synagogue Vězeňská 1
Robert Guttmann Gallery U Staré školy 3

METRO
Staroměstská

DISABLED ACCESS Only the Maisel Synagogue, Spanish Synagogue, Old Jewish Cemetery and Robert Guttman Gallery have disabled access.

SHOP Books and souvenirs are available at the gift shop in the foyer of the High Synagogue (Červená 4; opposite the Old-New Synagogue).

EAT There are numerous restaurants and cafés in Josefov

HIGHLIGHTS

13th-C portal with carved vine decoration	Old-New Synagogue
13th-C tympanum with leaf ornament	
Bema surrounded by Gothic grille	
14th-C tombstone of Rabbi Avigdor Karo	Old Jewish Cemetery
17th-C tombstone of Heudele Bassevi	
17th-C tombstone of Rabbi Löw	

Jews began settling in Prague from at least the 10th C onwards, but it was not until the mid-13th C that a ghetto emerged in the district around the Old-New Synagogue. Despite fires and pogroms, the ghetto flourished, its population rising to 7,000 by the 17th C. Renamed Josefov in honour of Emperor Joseph II, by 1850 the district had become an over-populated slum. Despite public protest, most of it was razed in 1895, leaving only buildings of historical interest still standing. The young Franz Kafka witnessed this traumatic event: 'The unhealthy old Jewish town within us', he once commented, 'is far more real than the hygienic town around us.'

The Nazis, far from wishing to destroy these surviving monuments, planned to turn them into a 'Museum of Jewry' to record for posterity the culture of a soon-to-be extinct race. A museum of Jewish art had existed since the early 20th C but, as a result of the Nazis' confiscation of Jewish property, its holdings expanded to become the largest collection of synagogal art in the world. The museum's growth coincided with the decimation of Czechoslovakia's Jewish population: a memorial in the Pinkas Synagogue records the names of 77,297 Jews killed during the Nazi occupation of the country.

Josefov is bisected by Pařížská, a grand tree-lined avenue lined with ornate turn-of-the-last-century apartment blocks, whose ground floors now accommodate stylish boutiques and a plethora of bars and restaurants. The district is today one of Prague's obligatory tourist sights, and there are often long queues to enter some of the monuments. To add to the confusion, because of recent flood damage some of the entry points have been relocated (to the Old Jewish Cemetery, for example), while other monuments, such as the Pinkas Synagogue, are currently closed for renovation.

OLD-NEW SYNAGOGUE

Situated just off Pařížská, the Old-New Synagogue (Staronová synagoga) is architecturally and historically the most important site of the former ghetto, and is Prague's most outstanding early-medieval building. Unfortunately, parts of it were damaged during the floods of 2002; a painstaking renovation programme is currently underway. It is the oldest functioning synagogue in Europe, dating back to the mid-13th C, and owes its unusual name to the fact that it was originally called the 'New Synagogue' until another, newer one was built in the vicinity. The narrow barrel-vaulted **vestibule** was originally the main hall, but became the women's gallery after the present hall was added in c. 1270. The metal boxes were added in the 17th C, placed in the vestibule for the collection of Jewish taxes.

The present **main hall**, one of the finest examples in Central Europe of the Cistercian Gothic style, is reached through a **13th-C portal** with an exquisitely carved vine tree bearing twelve bunches of grapes that refer to the twelve tribes of Israel (see picture opposite). There are numerous further references to the number twelve, both in the decoration and in the plan of the vaulted double-naved hall itself. Leaf ornamentation (13th-C) decorates the tympanum of the Torah shrine on the east wall.

In the middle of the hall stands a bema, surrounded by a beautiful Gothic grille; it was from here that the Jewish community's most famous son, Rabbi Löw, would read from the scrolls of the Torah (for more about Rabbi Löw, see p. 32). Above the bema hangs a flag donated to Prague's Jews in 1648 by the

אֶת הָאֱלֹהִים יְרָא
וְאֶת מִצְוֹתָיו שְׁמוֹר
כִּי זֶה כָּל הָאָדָם:

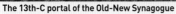

The 13th-C portal of the Old-New Synagogue

Emperor Ferdinand, who wanted to thank them for helping him fight off the Protestant Swedes. The benches lining the walls are early 19th-C, while on the walls themselves are traces of **medieval frescoes** and inscriptions (1618) from the Psalms.

OLD JEWISH CEMETERY

The Old Jewish Cemetery (Starý židovský hřbitov) is the Jewish Museum's most popular attraction. Though established in the late 15th C, some of the tombstones jumbled together here were transferred from an earlier cemetery. There are more than 12,000 tombstones, but graves are thought to be several deep because of a lack of space.

The tall, cracked and often perilously leaning stones are engraved with symbolic reliefs referring either to the occupation or the name of the deceased: for instance, a stag for someone named Hirsch, or a pair of scissors for a tailor. One of the most richly decorated stones is that of Heudele Bassevi (d. 1628), who was the wife of the first Prague Jew to be raised to the nobility; some of the other distinguished names include mayor Mordechaj Maisel (d. 1601), the astronomer David Gans (d. 1613), the scientist Josef Delmedigo (d. 1655) and the bibliophile David Oppenheim (d. 1736). The oldest stone is that of the **Rabbi Avigdor Karo** (d. 1389), while the last person to be buried here was Moses Beck in 1787.

Pebbles and scraps of paper with messages are often left on the graves as a gesture of respect towards the dead. The grave with the greatest accumulation of these is that of the most famous person to be buried here, **Rabbi Löw** (d. 1609), a renowned Talmudic scholar and a man of reputed supernatural powers. Numerous fanciful tales are told of Löw, but none more famous than that of his creation—from the mud of the Vltava—of Yossel the Golem. This sinister, Frankenstein-like figure inspired Gustav Meyrink's novel of 1915, *The Golem*, and the German Expressionist film of the same name by Paul Wegener. Since then, the mysterious golem has appeared in everything from 1960s horror film *It!* to Michael Chabon's 2000 bestseller, *The Amazing Adventures of Kavalier and Clay*.

OLD JEWISH CEMETERY

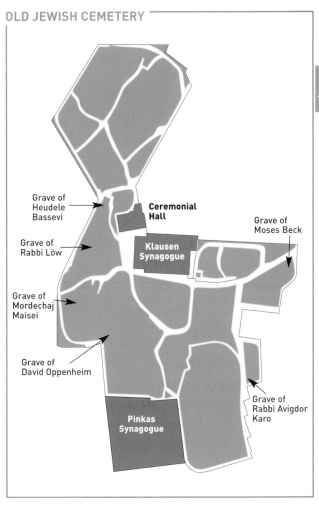

Grave of Heudele Bassevi

Ceremonial Hall

Grave of Moses Beck

Grave of Rabbi Löw

Klausen Synagogue

Grave of Mordechaj Maisei

Grave of David Oppenheim

Grave of Rabbi Avigdor Karo

Pinkas Synagogue

Prague's Jewish Cemetery

MAISEL SYNAGOGUE

Originally dating back to 1590, the building was given a neo-Gothic face lift at the end of the 19th C. It now contains an exhibition on the **history of the Jews in Bohemia and Moravia** up to the period of their emancipation in the 18th C. It covers the first Jewish settlements, medieval depictions of the Jewish community, and the changes brought about by Austrian Empress Maria Theresa's loosening of restrictions on Jews.

KLAUSEN SYNAGOGUE

The Klausen Synagogue, which stands by the entrance to the cemetery, was built in the late 16th C, but was destroyed by fire and had to be rebuilt in 1604. The stuccoed, barrel-vaulted interior contains a large collection of **manuscripts and prints**, as well as **silver and religious objects**. It is flanked on its western side by the neo-Romanesque **Ceremonial Hall**, built in 1906 for the Jewish Burial Society.

PINKAS SYNAGOGUE

Attached to the southern wall of the Old Jewish Cemetery, this 16th-C synagogue was turned into a Holocaust memorial after World War II. It closed following the floods of 2002, which destroyed the **wall inscriptions** listing the names and personal data of the 77,297 Jews killed by the Nazis in Bohemia and Moravia; the inscriptions are currently undergoing restoration. When the synagogue reopens, the exhibition will also include children's drawings depicting conditions at the Terezín ghetto near Prague, where many perished.

SPANISH SYNAGOGUE

This impressive neo-Moorish structure was built in 1882 for Prague's Sephardic community. Inside it is full of beautiful, vividly coloured floral patterns and stained glass, and has elaborate stucco decorations inspired by those of the Alhambra in Granada. On the ground floor and in the women's gallery is an exhibition on **the history of the Jews in Bohemia and Moravia**, which follows on from the exhibition in the Maisel Synagogue, taking the story up to 1945.

ROBERT GUTTMANN GALLERY

The gallery is a new venue that puts on temporary exhibitions of **19th- and 20th-C paintings** by Czech Jewish artists. Robert Guttman was born in 1880 and became known for his unconventional, expressive paintings and dreamy, eccentric lifestyle.

in the area

EAST OF THE OLD TOWN SQUARE

Powder Gate (Prašná brána) náměstí Republiky. Open daily in summer, 10 am–6 pm. A monumental entrance gate to the Old

Town, it marked the beginning of the Czech kings' coronation route; only later was it used as a storehouse for gunpowder (hence the name). It was built in the late 15th-C, but the turreted upper gallery, steeply pitched roof and flamboyant neo-Gothic decoration are the result of late-19th-C reconstruction work. *M* to náměstí Republiky **Map p. 9, 2C**

House of the Black Madonna (Dům U černé Matky Boží)/Museum of Czech Cubist Art Ovocný trh 19, 224 301 167, www.ngprague.cz. Open Tues–Sun, 10 am–6 pm. Built as a department store in 1911–12, this corner house is a fine example of Czech Cubism. Since 2003, the building has housed a small Museum of Czech Cubist Art administered by the National Gallery. *M* to náměstí Republiky or Můstek **Map p. 9, 1C**

Monastery Church of St James (sv. Jakuba) Malá Štupartská. Open Mon–Sat, 9.30 am–4 pm; Sun, 2 pm–4 pm. Founded in 1232, the church was completely remodelled in the late 17th C. Its enormously long and imposing interior has retained the medieval three-aisled plan and tall, Gothic proportions. Well worth attending is the sung High Mass on Sunday, which is followed by a free organ recital. *M* to náměstí Republiky **Map p. 9, 1B**

House of the Golden Ring (dům U zlatého prstenu)/Museum of 20th-C Czech Art Týnská 6. Open Tues–Sun, 10 am–6 pm. 224 827 022, www.citygalleryprague.cz. This long and rambling building, with its whitewashed vaulted rooms, provides the setting for the Prague City Gallery's comparatively small permanent exhibition of 20th-C Czech art (there's better to be seen at the Trade Fair Palace, see p. 131). Catalogues and books can be bought at the coffeehouse in the courtyard. *M* to Staroměstská **Map p. 9, 1B**

OLD TOWN SQUARE

Goltz-Kinský Palace (palác Kinských) Staroměstské náměstí 12. Open Tues–Sun, 10 am–6 pm. 224 810 758, www.ngprague.cz. One of Prague's most elegant Baroque palaces, designed by K.I. Dientzenhofer. In the late 19th C, part of the palace was turned into a state-run German-language secondary school, attended by Franz Kafka. The upper floors are now used for temporary exhibitions put on by the National Gallery. *M* to Staroměstská **Map p. 8, 4B**

House at the Stone Bell (Dům U kamenného zvonu) Staroměstské náměstí 13. Open Tues–Sun 10 am–6 pm. 222 327 677, www.citygalleryprague.cz. The Baroque cladding on this beautiful narrow-fronted building was recently removed to reveal the original mid-14th-C stonework. The interior, which features a small chapel with fragments of 14th-C murals, is used by the Prague City Gallery as an exhibition space and is the venue of the Zvon biennial for young Central European artists. *M* to Staroměstská **Map p. 8, 4B**

Kafka Museum U Radnice 5. Open Tues–Fri, 10 am–6 pm; Sat, 10 am–5 pm. On the little square (náměstí Franze Kafky) next to the Church of St Nicholas is the site of the house where Franz Kafka was born on July 3, 1883. The building, completely rebuilt in 1902 after a fire, now features a modest museum devoted to the writer, with photographs, quotations from his works and a display of first editions. *M* to Staroměstská **Map p. 8, 3B**

Church of St Nicholas (sv. Mikuláš) Staroměstské náměstí. Open Tues–Fri, 10 am–12 pm; Wed, 2 pm–4 pm. This fine example of Bohemian Baroque (1732–35) has an unusual design that was largely determined by the once-cramped nature of the site: the architectural elements have been elongated, which creates soaring proportions. The impressive, albeit spartan, interior boasts fine ceiling frescoes, but the painted decorations are subservient to the exceptionally rich stucco framework. *M* to Staroměstská **Map p. 8, 4B**

WEST OF THE OLD TOWN SQUARE
Czech Museum of Fine Arts (České muzeum výtvarných umění)
Husova 19–21. Open Tues–Sun, 10 am–6 pm. 222 220 218, www.cmvu.cz. From this year, the Museum's permanent collections will be displayed at the new Arts Centre in Kutná Hora, 60 km east of Prague, while this city gallery will host temporary exhibitions. It occupies three connected buildings at the junction of Karlova and Husova, the most elegant being the Renaissance

house at No. 21. The interior successfully incorporates the buildings' surviving medieval elements into a bright modern setting. *M* to Staroměstská **Map p. 8, 3C**

Clam-Gallas Palace Husova 20. Open Tues–Sun, 10 am–6 pm. 284 011 150, www.ahmp.cz/eng/gallas.html. A Baroque palace (1713–19) built by Johann Bernhard Fischer von Erlach, aided by the sculptor Matthias Braun and the Italian painter Carlo Carlone. The main façade, hemmed in on the narrow street, is in many ways remarkably Classical, yet it is given a dynamic Baroque quality by Braun's sculptural additions—the row of figures along the attic and, above all, the powerful, struggling atlantes supporting the two portals. The building is now home to the city archives, but temporary exhibitions (on Czech art and design) and classical concerts are occasionally held on the first floor, which is reached via a grand staircase with murals, stuccowork and views onto the courtyard. *M* to Staroměstská **Map p. 8, 3C**

Municipal Public Library Mariánské náměstí 1. Open Tues–Sun, 10 am–6 pm. 222 311 724, www.citygalleryprague.cz. A series of newly renovated rooms where temporary art exhibitions are put on by the Prague City Gallery. *M* to Staroměstská **Map p. 8, 2C**

Clementinum (Klementium) Mariánské náměstí (entrances also on Karlova and Křižovnická). Guided tours on the hour, Mon–Fri, 12 am–5 pm; Sat–Sun, 10 am–7 pm. This former Jesuit College is a vast complex of buildings encompassing four courtyards, several churches and chapels, and other sites. Most of it is taken up by the Czech National Library (Open Mon–Fri, 8 am–10 pm; Sat, 8 am–7 pm), which boasts the world's largest collection of works by the English religious reformer John Wycliffe. The 30-minute guided tour of the complex covers its two chief attractions: the Baroque library hall (Barokní sál), a sumptuous gilded space of 1727, and the 52-metre-high observatory tower, with magnificent views of Prague. *M* to Staroměstská **Map p. 8, 2C**

Puppet Museum (Muzeum loutek) Karlova 12. Open Tues–Sun, 12 am–8 pm. 222 220 913, www.puppetart.com. In Gothic cellars, the museum traces the history of Czech puppetry from the 17th C to the 19th C, with many fine examples on show. *M* to Staroměstská **Map p. 8, 2C**

SOUTH OF THE OLD TOWN SQUARE

**Náprstek Museum of Asian, African and American Cultures
(Nápstrkovo muzeum asijských, afrických a amerických kultur)**
Betlémské náměstí 1. Open Tues–Sun, 9 am–5.30 pm. 224 497
500, www.aconet.cz/npm/eindex.html. This ethnographical
museum was founded in the 19th C by the industrialist and
adventurer Vojta Náprstek (1826–94). *M* to Národní třída **Map p. 8,
3D**

Bethlehem Chapel (Betlémská kaple) Betlémské náměstí. Open
April–Oct, Tues–Sun 10 am–6.30 pm; Nov–March, 10 am–5.30 pm.
224 248 595. This austere, twin-gabled chapel is famous largely
on account of its association with the religious reformer Jan Hus
(see p. 14), who preached from its pulpit in the 15th C. The box-
like interior, reconstructed in 1950–52, has pseudo-medieval wall
paintings mixed up with restored 14th-C fragments of Biblical
scenes. The first floor has a display on the history of the Hussite
movement. *M* to Národní třída **Map p. 8, 3D**

JEWISH QUARTER

Rudolfinum (Alšovo nábřeží) náměstí Jana Palacha 12. Open
Tues–Fri, 10 am–6 pm. 227 059 346, www.galerierudolfinum.cz.
This imposing neo-Renaissance building was built between 1875
and 1884, originally for use as an art gallery and concert hall,
before serving as the seat of the Czechoslovak parliament in the
inter-war period. Today it hosts the Prague Spring Festival, and is
also one of the city's best venues for contemporary art, with
shows held in natural light that illuminates the Rudolfinum
Gallery. *M* to Staroměstská **Map p. 8, 2B**

Museum of Decorative Arts (Umělecko průmyslové muzeum) 17.
listopadu 2. Open Tues–Sun, 10 am–6 pm. 251 093 111. Founded
in 1885, this museum is one of the great little-known attractions
of Prague. The main permanent display—unpromisingly called
'Stories of Materials'—includes a superlative collection of
Meissen porcelain figurines, as well as Bohemian Baroque glass,
furniture, metalwork, clocks, textiles, costumes, prints, posters
and photographs. The exhibits are housed in rooms decorated
with turn-of-the-20th-C grotesque work, and the layout is

endearingly old-fashioned and crowded. The overall effect is of great wealth and variety. **M** to Staroměstská **Map p. 8, 3B**

commercial galleries

Art Master Gallery Týnská ulička 5 and Liliová 6, 777 082 645, www.inmodern.com. Open 10 am–7 pm. Contemporary works by Ukrainian, Armenian, Russian and Georgian artists. **M** to Staroměstská **Map p. 8, 4B** and **3C**

Bayer & Bayer Řetězová 7, 222 220 029, www.galerie-bayer.cz. Open Tues–Sat, 12 pm– 6 pm. Upstairs from the Café Montmartre, works by mainly middle-generation Czech artists are displayed in two beautiful rooms with painted beamed ceilings. **M** to Staroměstská **Map p. 8, 3C**

Galerie Behémot Elišky Krásnohorské 6, 222 317 829. Open Tues–Sat, 10 am–6 pm. Contemporary works by Czech and Slovak artists of the pre- and post-1989 generation. The focus is on installations, some of which are created inside the gallery. The exhibitions are usually high standard and change regularly. **M** to Staroměstská **Map p. 8, 4B**

Galerie Hollar Smetanovo nábřeží 6, 224 235 243, www.hollar.cz. Open Tues–Sun, 10 am–1 pm and 2 pm–6 pm. Founded in 1917, the gallery is housed in the Charles University's Faculty of Sociology. It specialises in 20th-C Czech graphic art, with a new exhibition held each month. Many of the prints are for sale. **M** to Národní třída **Map p. 8, 2D**

Galerie Jakubská Jakubská 4, 224 827 926, www.galeriejakubska.cz. Open Mon–Sat, 10 am–6 pm. Impressionist paintings by the Ukrainian Alexandr Onishenko, who began his career in the Czech Republic as a street artist working on the Charles Bridge. The gallery also sells contemporary works by other Ukrainian and Russian artists. **M** to náměstí Republiky **Map p. 9, 1B**

Galerie Jiřího a Běly Kolářových Betlémské náměstí 8, 222 220 689. Open daily, 10 am–7 pm. The private gallery of Jiří Kolář, one of the most famous contemporary Czech artists, who began his career as a banned poet in the 1950s before going on to produce witty surrealistic collages involving words, images and political comment. The gallery sells work by

Jiří, his wife Běla, and the couple's many friends and colleagues. *M* to Národní třída **Map p. 8, 3D**

Galerie La Femme Bílkova 2, 224 812 656, www.glf.cz (in Czech). Open daily, 11 am–7 pm. A small gallery founded in 2000. It's devoted, as its name suggests, to the theme of women expressed in paintings, sculptures and graphic art. *M* to Staroměstská **Map p. 8, 4A**

Jewish Art Gallery Maiselova 7, 602 386 193, www.jewishgallery.cz. Open 10 am–7 pm. Oil paintings—mainly landscapes, still lifes and Prague cityscapes—by the Russian Jewish émigré artist Michael Sloutsker. *M* to Staroměstská **Map p. 8, 3B**

Parnas – Viktor Safonkin Jáchymova 2, 224 23 94 76, www.euro surrealism.com. Open Mon–Fri, 10 am–7 pm; Sat–Sun, 12 pm–6 pm. Strange and vivid artworks in the European surrealist and symbolist traditions. *M* to Staroměstská **Map p. 8, 3B**

Prague House of Photography (Pražský dům fotografie) Haštalská 1, 224 810 779, www.php-gallery.cz. Open daily, 11 am–6 pm. The PHP puts on excellent monthly exhibitions of classic and contemporary photography from the Czech Republic and abroad. Visitors can purchase prints (made from the original glass negatives) by such pioneers of the art form as Jaromír Funke and František Drtikol (the latter specialising in female nudes in disturbing, geometrical settings). *M* to náměstí Republiky **Map p. 9, 1A**

U Prstenu Jilská 14, 224 22 28 64, www.uprstenu.cz (in Czech). Open daily 11 am–7 pm. Paintings, lithographs, jewellery and much else, all by local artists. Charming café on-site. *M* to Staroměstská or Národní třída **Map p. 8, 3C**

eat

The Old Town has restaurants of every category. it's a good idea to book ahead if you're eating at one of the more popular establishments. But don't be afraid to venture a little further in search of a good meal—the further you get from the hordes of tourists, the calmer (and cheaper) your experience will be.

RESTAURANTS

€ **Chez Marcel** Haštalská 12, 22 315 670. This French bistro serves inexpensive lunches and a very reasonable selection of wines in a pleasant Old Town setting. *M* to Staroměstská or náměstí Republiky **Map p. 9, 1B**

Country Life Melantrichova 15, 224 213 366. Without doubt, this is the best place for vegetarian snacks in the vicinity of Old Town Square. Country Life offers self-service hot and cold dishes, tasty organic soups and salads, freshly squeezed fruit juices and, best of all, smoke-free rooms and a dispenser with filtered water. *M* to Staroměstská or Můstek **Map p. 8, 4C**

Klub Architektů Betlémské náměstí 5A, 224 401 214. In the courtyard opposite the entrance to the Bethlehem Chapel (see p. 39). Expect no more than a basic stomach filler. *M* to Národní třída or Můstek **Map p. 8, 3D**

Pizzeria Roma Due Liliová 18, 222 714 154. This convenient 24-hour snack bar serves pizzas, calzone, and Gambrinus on tap. *M* to Staroměstská **Map p. 8, 3C**

€€ **Kogo** Havelská 27, 224 214 543. This is a good place for fresh salads and pastas. Lunch and dinner find a bustling crowd of punters enjoying innovative pizzas and a decent wine list. Stop here before visiting the open-air market on the same street. There are also two other branches of Kogo in Prague. The dining space almost doubles in summer when an attached outdoor courtyard opens. *M* to Můstek **Map p. 8, 4C**

Le Saint-Jacques Jakubská 4, 222 322 685. This is an excellent little French restaurant with a comfortably elegant candlelit interior and live piano music most nights. *M* to náměstí Republiky **Map p. 9, 1B**

Red Hot & Blues Jakubská 12, 222 323 364. A favourite expat bar, as can be seen immediately by the Czech and American flags above the entrance. The Tex-Mex and Cajun-style food is of dubious quality and authenticity, but the raucous blues nights sort of compensate. There is a small patio within. *M* to náměstí Republiky **Map p. 9, 1B**

Reykjavík Karlova 20, 222 221 218. Centrally located on the 'Royal Route', the Reykjavík specialises in seafood flown in fresh from Iceland, homeland of owner Thorir Gunnarsson. It's essentially glorified fish and chips, but of exceptionally good quality and made the traditional Icelandic way. *M* to Staroměstská **Map p. 8, 2C**

Stoleti Karoliny Světlé 21, 222 220 008. Stoleti is situated in the southern part of the Old Town, well away from the crowds. This unpretentious establishment serves decent Czech fare and good salads at very reasonable prices. Memorably, they have a salmon dish named after Gloria Swanson (other stars are honoured with further menu items). *M* to Národní třída **Map p. 8, 2D**

€€€ Flambée Husova 5, 224 248 512. This is a top-of-the-range establishment serving game and seafood dishes in a vaulted medieval cellar. It's ridiculously expensive, but considering it lists Tom Cruise and Michael Jackson among its former guests, that is hardly surprising. The menu changes seasonally; expect meat-based dishes, but more in the tradition of French than Czech cuisine. Although tasting menus are an option, the finely chosen à la carte menu includes an exquisite sampling of foie gras, lobster tails and caviar. *M* to Staroměstská or Národní třída **Map p. 8, 3C**

Pravda Pařížská 17, 222 326 203. This newly revamped and touristy establishment is located in the heart of the Jewish Quarter. The food is cosmopolitan and the staff attentive. *M* to Staroměstská **Map p. 8, 3B**

Rybí trh Týn 5, 224 895 447. You can find Rybí trh in the busy courtyard (Ungelt) between Malá Štupartská and Týnská. Saltwater and freshwater fish specialities prepared to order are what most of the diners come for. It's good if you're in the area, but there's nothing to rival Kampa Park (see p. 100). *M* to Staroměstská **Map p. 9, 1B**

U Červeného Kola Anežská 2, 224 811 118. This is a charming restaurant with a summer garden in a peaceful part of town. The 15th-C building it occupies was once part of St Agnes Convent (see p. 22). The menu is traditional Czech. *M* to náměstí Republiky **Map p. 9, 1A**

CAFÉS & TEAHOUSES

Blatouch Vězeňská 4. This is a serious, bookcase-lined student café. Blatouch has secluded seating in the mezzanine area as well as a delightful small patio at the back. *M* to Staroměstská **Map p. 8, 4B**

Dahab Dlouhá 33. A uniquely decorated tearoom with a Middle Eastern theme. At night it's populated by refugees from the Roxy club next door. There's a vast array of teas to choose from, but the main selling points are the serene ambience and comfortable seating. *M* to Staroměstská **Map p. 8, 4B**

Franz Kafka Café Široká 12. This café pulls in the tourists on account of its Kafka theme and memorabilia, but the lunches are a bit disappointing. Its location makes it useful, though, when visiting the Jewish Quarter. *M* to Staroměstská **Map p. 8, 3B**

Le Patio Haštalská 18 (corner of Rybná). A very chic café, with prices to match, decked out in shades of orange. It has an adjoining, tastefully appointed shop that sells things for the home. *M* to Staroměstská or náměstí Republiky **Map p. 9, 1B**

Café Milena Staroměstské náměstí 22. This is a passable pastiche of the sort of café Kafka might have frequented, and it's named after his great love (and translator), the journalist Milena Jesenská. *M* to Staroměstská **Map p. 8, 4C**

Café Montmartre Řetězová 7. This used to be one of Prague's raunchiest meeting places in the early 20th C. Now its erstwhile Bohemian spirit is firmly dead and buried, but it's worth a look if you happen to be passing. *M* to Staroměstská **Map p. 8, 3C**

Nostress Café Dušní 10. Just a street away from the major sites in the Jewish Quarter, this café and gallery is a relaxed, no-stress choice for a light lunch. A small menu of tapas, soups and salads is perfect for refueling. Check out the silk flowers and other housewares in the attached gallery on the way out. *M* to Staroměstská **Map p. 8, 4B**

Týnská Literární kavárna Týnská 6. In a pleasant courtyard with wicker chairs, this arty café is frequented by Charles University students and visitors to the gallery inside the House of the Golden Ring (see p. 36). *M* to Staroměstská **Map p. 9, 1B**

U Prstenu Jilská 14. This is a pleasant café with an appealing pre-war feel, situated in a tiny courtyard. In addition, there is an adjoining art gallery (see p. 41). *M* to Staroměstská or Národní třída **Map p. 8, 3C**

shop

There are tourist shops selling Czech crystal and garnets all over Prague, so shop around to get the best price. Lovely and inexpensive black and white photos of Prague are sold by vendors on the Charles Bridge, and make a nice souvenir or gift. The most fashionable high street is Pařížská , which connects the Old Town Square with the Vltava, bisecting the Jewish Quarter. The area to the east is home to a few new fashion designers and some interesting, offbeat stores.

ANTIQUES

Art Deco Galerie Michalská 21, 224 22 30 76. This shop sells applied art from the 1920s and 1930s. There's a large choice of glass and porcelain, some especially fine hats and dresses, and jewellery, clocks, furniture and other curiosities. *M* to Staroměstská or Můstek **Map p. 8, 4C**

Dorotheum Ovocní trh 2, 224 222 001. This long-established upmarket antiques shop and auction house focuses mainly on 19th- and 20th-C glassware, porcelain, paintings, jewellery and household items. It's a branch of the very reputable Vienna-based Dorotheum house. *M* to Můstek or náměstí Republiky **Map p. 9, 1C**

Papilio Antiques Týn 1, 224 895 454. This antiques shop and auction house specialises in Biedermeier furniture, Art Nouveau silverware, and other fine antiques. However, the real attraction is the Loetz Bohemian glass—Papilio has one of the richest collections in Europe. *M* to Staroměstská or náměstí Republiky **Map p. 9, 1B**

BOOKS

Anagram Týn 4, 224 895 737. This is one of the best places in Prague to pick up second-hand English-language books on subjects ranging from history, photography and fiction (including Czech works in translation) to art and architecture, science and health. There is also an impressively large selection of children's books. The staff are very helpful. *M* to náměstí Republiky **Map p. 9, 1B**

Big Ben Bookshop Malá Štupartská 5, 224 826 565. This friendly English-language bookshop is situated opposite the Church of St James (see p. 34). Big Ben offers a wide selection of bestsellers, travel guides and children's books, as well as newspapers and magazines. *M* to náměstí Republiky **Map p. 9, 1B**

Knihkupectví Franze Kafky Staroměstské náměstí 12, 222 321 454. This excellent bookshop is located in what was once the premises of the Kafka family's haberdashery business. It sells travel literature, academic books, coffee table albums and much else. *M* to Staroměstská **Map p. 8, 4C**

Knihkupectví U Černé Matky Boží Celetná 34, 224 211 275. A specialist art bookshop located on the ground floor of the House of the Black Madonna (see p. 36). If you're looking to buy a gift, then this is the place. *M* to náměstí Republiky **Map p. 9, 1C**

CLOTHES

Bohéme Dušní 8, 224 813 840. The Czech designer boutique Bohéme specialises in knitted garments, leatherwear and accessories for women. The look is comfortable, almost cosy, but without sacrificing a distinct high-fashion touch. *M* to Staroměstská **Map p. 8, 4B**

Dessous-Dessus Králodvorská 7, 224 811 779. This shop sells sexy upmarket lingerie, but wearable stuff rather than adventurously trashy designs. *M* to náměstí Republiky **Map p. 9, 2B**

Ivana Follová Týn 1 (Ungelt) 224 895 460. Fashion designer Follová is very fond of silk, which she dyes in unique patterns. Her style is dramatic and free, with ethnic influences. Lots of hand-made, high-quality accessories, including glass beads, scarves, hats, sunglasses and silk dresses. *M* to Staroměstská or náměstí Republiky **Map p. 8, 4B**

Tatiana Dušní 1, 224 813 723. The store of a designer Czech label for women. The shop mostly sells exclusive Czech collections. The look is slightly grown-up, but still sexy and Bond-girl-esque. *M* to Staroměstská **Map p. 8, 4B**

Wilvorst U Prašné brány 1-3, 222 323 573. Luxury mens and womenswear from René Lezard, Joop, Marc O'Polo and others. *M* to náměstí Republiky **Map p. 9, 2B**

FOOD & WINE

Country Life Melantrichova 15, 224 213 366. This is an excellent health-food shop just a short walk from the Old Town Square. The on-site self-service restaurant (see p. 42) is a haven for vegetarians. *M* to Můstek or Staroměstská **Map p. 8, 4C**

Fruits de France Jindřišská 9, 224 220 304. This shop has fresh produce flown in from France. The fruit and vegetables are excellent, as are the French cheeses, sausages, chocolate, wine and brandy. Deli snacks are served on-site if all the good stuff tempts your appetite. *M* to Můstek **Map p. 9, 2D**

Havelský Market Havelská. With its pleasant Old Town setting, this is one of Prague's best open-air markets. Ignore the tacky souvenir stalls and head straight for the fruit and veg, but beware of pickpockets. It's also a good place to buy flowers. *M* to Národní třída or Můstek **Map p. 8, 4C**

Monarch Na Perštýně 15, 224 239 602. This wine shop is run by an importer, and has excellent Czech and New World wines that can be sampled on-site or shipped anywhere you want. In spite of the fact that it's Czech beer that always gets the attention, since 1989 much effort has gone into improving Czech wines, and it's a fun way to do a virtual tour of the country. The finest Czech wines are from Southern Moravia, with excellent Ruländer, Sauvignon, Traminer and Spätburgunder wines from Velké Pavlovice, Mikulov, Musov and Znojmo. *M* to Národní třída **Map p. 8, 3D**

GLASS, CERAMICS & CRAFTS

The emergence of Bohemian crystal began in the 16th C, under the reign of Rudolph II. Cutting and engraving became Bohemian specialities, and by the beginning of the 18th C, Bohemian glass was famous worldwide, having stolen a march on Venetian glass. Lead crystal production in England and elsewhere cut into Bohemia's dominance, but in the 20th C the industry began to revive. Today, Bohemian crystal is a popular tourist buy, and decorative glass has seen a new revival also.

Celetná Crystal Celetná 15, 222 324 022. This vast glass emporium is spread over three floors. It has a mind-boggling assortment of top-of-the-range Bohemian lead crystal (24%) as well as porcelain, garnet jewellery and lower-end lead crystal (10%). *M* to Staroměstská **Map p. 9, 1C**

Karlovarský porcelán Pařížská 12, 224 811 023. The store carries high-quality decorative and functional porcelain produced in the Western Bohemian spa town of Karlovy Vary. *M* to Staroměstská **Map p. 8, 4B**

Kubista Ovocný trh 19, 224 236 378. Set on the ground floor of the House of the Black Madonna (see p. 36), Kubista sells reproductions of Cubist applied art as well as some fine (and very expensive) original pieces. Cubism was widely embraced by Czech artists of the 1920s, and these applied-art variations are well worth seeing. *M* to náměstí Republiky or Můstek **Map p. 9, 1C**

Moser Glass Na příkopě 12 and Malé náměstí 11, 224 211 293, 221 611 520. Established in 1857, Moser is the oldest Bohemian glass manufacturer and specialises in engraved glassware. The company pioneered a manufacturing technique using potash instead of lead, meaning its products are more ecologically sound (and more expensive) than lead crystal, though as hard and brilliant. *M* to Můstek (for Na příkopě branch) or Staroměstská (for Malé náměstí branch) **Map p. 9, 1C** and **Map 8, 4C**

Rott Crystal Malé náměstí 3, 224 229 529. The famous shop front, decorated with figurative and ornamental designs by Mikoláš Aleš, still bears the name of the original owner—the ironmongery firm of V. J. Rott. Nowadays, Rott sells some of the best quality Bohemian crystal (24% lead content) as well as garnet jewellery and a wide selection of porcelain. *M* to Staroměstská **Map p. 8, 4C**

Slovimex Betlémské náměstí 2, 222 220 521. Slovimex offers a wide range of filigree products made according to traditional techniques—everything from mouth-blown Soda potash glass to hand-cut and hand-painted lead crystal. *M* to Národní třída or Můstek **Map p. 8, 3D**

JEWELLERY

Carollinum Pařížská 11, 224 252 203. This store has some designs of its own, and also carries a large selection of brands like Rolex, Cartier, Van Cleef & Arpels, Piaget, Chopard, etc. *M* to Staroměstská **Map p. 8, 4B**

Galerie Vlasta Staroměstské náměstí 5, 222 3 8 119. The gallery sells the intricate gold and silver wire jewellery made by award-winning artist Vlasta Wasserbauerová, whose distinct, ethereal style is instantly recognisable. *M* to Staroměstská **Map p. 8, 4C**

Granát Turnov Dlouhá 30, 222 315 612. The co-operative that owns this shop is the biggest player in the Czech Republic's garnet industry, and this is definitely the place to come if you're looking for jewellery with this fiery red, classic stone. *M* to Staroměstská **Map p. 8, 4B**

MUSIC

Philharmonia Pařížská 13, 22 324 060. The City of Prague Philharmonic Orchestra is a busy recording orchestra, well-known for its work on film scores. This, the official shop of the orchestra, has a wide selection of classical music CDs and recordings from around the world. *M* to Staroměstská **Map p. 8, 4B**

Pohodlí Benediktská 7, 224 827 028. This tiny shop specialises in world music. The service is very friendly. *M* to náměstí Republiky **Map p. 9, 2B**

PRAGUE CASTLE &
THE HRADČANY

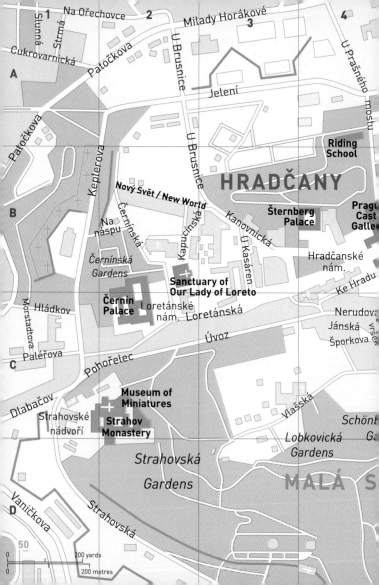

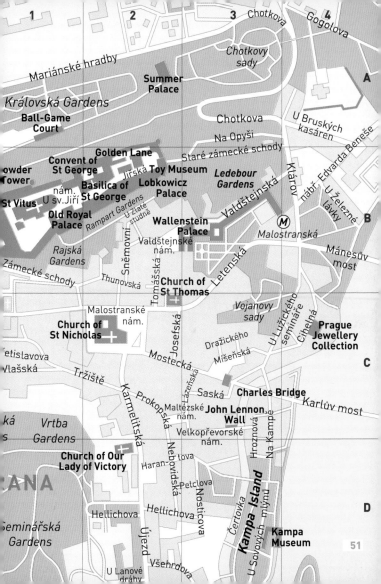

1   **2**   **3**   **4**

Chotkova   Gogolova

Chotkovy sady

Mariánské hradby

A

Královská Gardens

Summer Palace

Ball-Game Court

Chotkova

Na Opyši

U Bruských kasáren

Staré zámecké schody

Golden Lane

Convent of St George

Jirská   **Toy Museum**

Ledebour Gardens

Klárov

nábř. Edvarda Beneše

owder ower

Basilica of St George

nám.   **Lobkowicz Palace**

U železné lávky

St Vitus

U sv. Jiří

Valdštejnská

B

Old Royal Palace

Rampart Gardens   U Zlaté studně

Wallenstein Palace

Ⓜ

Malostranská

Rajská Gardens

Sněmovní

Valdštejnské nám.

Mánesův most

Zámecké schody

Thunovská

Letenská

Tomášská

Church of St Thomas

Malostranské nám.

Vojanovy sady

Church of St Nicholas

Josefská

U Lužického semináře

Cihelná

Prague Jewellery Collection

C

řetislavova

Vlašská

Tržiště

Mostecká

Dražického

Míšeňská

Lázeňská

Saská

Charles Bridge

Karlův most

ká s

Vrtba Gardens

Prokopská

Karmelitská

Maltézské nám.

John Lennon Wall

Hroznová

Na Kampě

Velkopřevorské nám.

Church of Our Lady of Victory

Nebovidská

Haranova

Pelclova

Nosticova

Čertovka

Kampa Island

D

ANA

Hellichova

Hellichova

Újezd

emiriářská Gardens

U Sovových mlýnů

Kampa Museum

51

U Lanové dráhy

Všehrdova

Prague Castle, the largest ancient castle in the world, rises above the Little Quarter like a classic picture-postcard image, its lofty Gothic spires dominating the city's skyline. The Hrad's ancient origins predate even Prague itself, and more than any other monument in the Czech Republic it has come to symbolise the changing fortunes of the Czech nation.

Bohemia's first rulers installed themselves here in the 9th C, and today it is the official residence of the President of the Republic. Over the centuries, great dynasties of rulers all left their mark on the Castle, which in part explains the dizzying mix of architectural styles that confronts visitors. Indeed, the Castle's elegant Classical casing encompasses an astonishing array of monuments. Foremost among these are the Cathedral of St Vitus, the burial place of Bohemia's saints and monarchs; the Prague Castle Gallery, housing the remnants of Rudolf II's superb art collection; and the toy-like Golden Lane, where Kafka once lived and worked.

The traditional approach to the Castle is along Nerudova street, which rises gently up the hill towards Hradčany Square, following the processional route of Bohemia's kings; the quickest ascent is up the Old Castle Steps (Staré zámecké schody), which begin at a point just to the north of Malostranská station, and enter the citadel at its narrow eastern end. There is so much to see at the Castle that the better part of a day is required to begin to do it justice. To conserve their energy, many visitors prefer to reach the site by public transport and save the beautiful walks through the Little Quarter for the afternoon descent.

THE CASTLE (PRAŽSKY HRAD)

OPEN	**Historic buildings** open daily. April–Oct, 9 am–5 pm; Nov–March, 9 am–4 pm. **Grounds** open daily. April–Oct, 5 am–12 am; Nov–March, 5 am–11 pm. **Gardens** open daily. April–Oct, 10 am–6 pm; Nov–March closed
CHARGES	You are free to walk through the castle grounds and its three courtyards, but you will need a ticket to enter any of the buildings. These can be purchased any of the entrances, but a cheaper and more convenient option is to buy one of the special tickets (A, B or C) covering groups of buildings within the castle complex:

Ticket A (350/175 Kč) Covers St Vitus's Cathedral (chancel, royal crypt, tower; entrance to the nave is free), Powder Tower, Basilica of St George, Old Royal Palace, Golden Lane

Ticket B (220/110 Kč) Covers St Vitus's Cathedral (chancel, royal crypt, tower; entrance to the nave is free), Old Royal Palace, Golden Lane

Ticket C (50 Kč) Covers Golden Lane

These special tickets are available from the Prague Castle Information Centre in the Third Courtyard. Choosing which ticket to buy depends on how much time you have to spare. To see all the sites on Ticket A, for instance, would require at least half a day, while Golden Lane (Ticket C) can be visited in less than an hour.

There are also several important sites within the castle complex that are run by different institutions and are therefore not covered by the above tickets. These sites include the **Prague Castle Gallery** (Second Courtyard, see p. 64), **Convent of St George** (náměstí U sv. Jiří; see p. 67), the **Toy Museum** (Jiřská; see p. 78), the **Historical Museum** (Lobkowicz Palace; see p. 78) and the **Royal Riding School** (U Prašného mostu; see p. 78). Tickets for these buildings can be bought at their respective entrances. Prices and hours vary.

TELEPHONE	**Prague Castle Information Centre** 224 373 368, 224 372 434-5 **Prague Castle Shop** 224 373 521
WEB	www.hrad.cz
MAIN ENTRANCE	Hradčanské náměstí
METRO	Malostranská, then No. 22 tram to the junction of Mariánské hradby and U Prašného mostu; if travelling by taxi, ask to be dropped off on Hradčanské náměstí (Hradčany Square)

DISABLED ACCESS St. Vitus Cathedral (including toilets), Basilica of St. George, Old Royal Palace (Vladislav Hall entrance), Prague Castle Gallery, Golden Lane, Prague Castle Gardens, Ball-Game Court, Royal Riding School

SHOP The Prague Castle Information Centre (Third Courtyard) sells tickets, audio-guides (250 Kč, 3 hours), maps and has an ATM. You can also book guided tours here (1 hour; 80 Kč per person, minimum 5 people; Tue–Sun, 9 am–4 pm). The Prague Castle Shop in the Chapel of the Holy Rood (Second Courtyard) sells books and souvenirs, as well as tickets for concerts, exhibitions and other events, but does not sell tickets to the historic buildings within the castle complex.

The history of Prague's citadel goes back to the 9th C, when it became the first seat of the Přemyslid dynasty, but the citadel would not reach its zenith until the reign of Charles IV (1344–78), who made his imperial residence here and ordered the construction of the great Gothic cathedral of St Vitus. This period of intense building activity was cut short in 1420 with the outbreak of the Hussite Wars, and was not renewed until the reign of Vladislav the Jagiellon (1471–1516), who brought the German architect Benedikt Ried to Prague to rebuild and extend the castle's palace and fortifications.

In the 16th C, Bohemia's Habsburg rulers transformed the citadel into an impressive Renaissance complex, with Italianate structures such as the **Summer Palace (Belvedere)** and **Ball-Game Court**. Rudolph II (1576–1611) gathered here an international group of scientific and artistic luminaries, and the castle once again became, if only briefly, the seat of one of Europe's most brilliant courts. His successor, Matthias (1611–19), vaunted the glories of the Habsburgs through the commissioning of the imposing triumphal arch known today as the **Matthias Gateway**, but the political consequences of the Thirty Years War reduced the castle to the status of a secondary residence, and it subsequently fell into decline. Little important work was carried out until the reign of Maria Theresa (1740–80), who initiated a major rebuilding campaign that gave the complex the late-Baroque and neo-Classical framework that it has largely kept to this day.

The towers of the Cathedral of St Vitus

The last important building campaign in the castle took place after 1918, when Tomáš Masaryk turned the complex into the presidential seat of the newly created Republic of Czechoslovakia. **St Vitus's Cathedral** was finally finished. Later in the 20th C, the castle acquired sinister connotations, thanks partially to its popular identification with the famous novel by Franz Kafka, who worked here after 1916 in a house rented by his sister on **Golden Lane**. Kafka's vision of faceless tyranny and monstrous bureaucracy seems to have been prophetic of the years when the castle served as the seat of Czechoslovakia's Communist rulers.

CATHEDRAL OF ST VITUS

HIGHLIGHTS
14th-C Golden Portal
14th-C portrait heads in the chancel
Wenceslas Chapel

CATHEDRAL OF ST VITUS

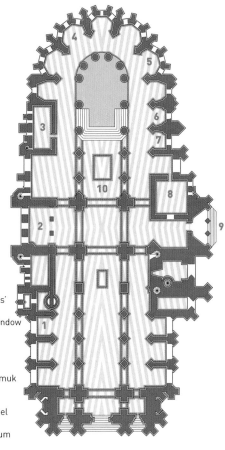

1. New Archbishops'
   Chapel, Mucha
   stained-glass window
2. Organ loft
3. Old Sacristy
4. Jerusalem
   candelabrum
5. St John of Nepomuk
6. Royal Oratory
7. Stairs to crypt
8. Wenceslas Chapel
9. Golden Portal
10. Royal Mausoleum

St Vitus's is one of the finest and most richly endowed cathedrals in Central Europe. It is pre-Romanesque in origin, but the present Gothic structure was begun in 1344 by the French architect Matthew of Arras, whom Charles IV summoned from the papal court at Avignon. Matthew's work was continued by the brilliant Petr Parléř, who completed the east end, enlarged the St Wenceslas chapel, constructed the exquisite south portal, and began work on the nave. When the Hussites occupied the castle in 1421, the cathedral was greatly damaged and many of its furnishings destroyed. Building activity was only resumed towards the end of the 15th C, beginning with the strange **Royal Oratory** put up in the south side of the ambulatory.

Vladislav the Jagiellon's principal architect was the great Benedikt Ried. He formulated grandiose plans for the completion of the nave, but these were abandoned in 1511 because of a lack of funds. The main additions to the cathedral later in the century were the work of Bonifác Wohlmut, who was responsible for the **Renaissance organ loft** in the north transept and for crowning the Gothic south tower with a Renaissance gallery and bulbous domes. Further attempts to complete the nave were thwarted, and it was not until the formation in 1861 of the 'Union for the Completion of the Cathedral' that work was begun in earnest to try to finish the building. This new campaign, headed by Josef Mocker, saw the introduction of many pseudo-Gothic elements. The fabric of the building was finally completed in 1929.

EXTERIOR

The high point of the exterior is undoubtedly the **south façade**— the work of Petr Parléř, who wanted to give particular emphasis to the side of the building that housed St Wenceslas's tomb and faced the city. This façade is dominated by its **96-metre-high tower**. It has a main window protected by a wonderfully intricate gilded Renaissance grille. Immediately to the right of the tower are the three arches of Petr Parléř's south porch or **'Golden Portal'**, which is decorated on the outside with a much-restored

Alfons Mucha Detail from *Lives of Sts Cyril and Methodius* (1931)

mosaic of the Last Judgement executed in the late 14th C by Venetian artists. One of Parléř's main contributions to the cathedral was his inventive **vaulting**, as can be seen inside the porch, where a skeletal system of ribs is spread out like a fan. Above the porch, to the right, is a further example of Parléř's structural daring—an openwork staircase of startling complexity.

INTERIOR

The plan and proportions of the building clearly reflect the work of a French architect, and indeed the arrangement of the east end, with its radiating chapels, seems to have been inspired by Narbonne Cathedral. Petr Parléř provided the chancel with its elegant vaulting system of parallel diagonal ribs and also began the triforium, which runs round the whole building. Inside it is a celebrated series of **portrait heads** (so high up they can scarcely be seen) representing all those involved in the building of the cathedral, including Parléř himself and members of Charles IV's family. The whole west end of the nave is a lifeless imitation of the east end, and bears little relation to the ambitious structure that Benedikt Ried would have created. The finest of the modern contributions to the building are the **stained-glass windows**, executed mainly by František Kysela and Max Švabinský. The latter's largest work here is the *Last Judgement* window in the south transept.

NAVE

The finest of the nave chapels is the third on the left-hand side, the **New Archbishops' Chapel**, which has been the burial place of Prague's archbishops since 1909 and also houses the tomb of the art historian bishop Antonín Podlaha (his research played an important part in the last phase of the cathedral's construction). The chapel is adorned with a vivid stained-glass window by **Alfons Mucha** of the *Lives of Sts Cyril and Methodius* (see picture opposite). Attached to the north wall of the north transept is Bonifác Wohlmut's curious **organ loft** (1557–61), which combines a harmonious Renaissance front with Gothic vaulting inside.

AMBULATORY

The **Old Sacristy**, at the northwestern end of the ambulatory, is notable mainly for its vaulting—a dramatically suspended boss supported by four skeletal ribs—begun by Parléř in 1356. Tombs from the Parléř workshop (1370s) of prominent members of the Přemyslid dynasty are in three of the radiating chapels in the apse; the first contains the so-called **Jerusalem candelabrum**, a fine example of Rhenish craftsmanship of the early 12th C. Another remarkable tomb from the Parléř workshop—a **marble effigy of Jan Očko of Vlašim** (1370)—is in the Chapel of St John of Nepomuk.

The **tomb of St John of Nepomuk** (1736) is unquestionably the finest of the Baroque furnishings in the cathedral. It is an elaborate silver structure under a canopy hung with draperies supported by angels, designed by Johann Bernhard Fischer von Erlach, and stands in the ambulatory passage.

One of the more remarkable additions to the ambulatory is the **Royal Oratory**—a balcony decorated with characteristic late-Gothic fantasy and naturalism, imitating the branches of a tree; this highly entertaining work, dating back to the early years of Vladislav the Jagiellon's reign, is sometimes attributed to the Frankfurt sculptor Hans Spiess. Inside the Chapel of St Andrew is the tombstone of Jaroslav von Martinic (d. 1649), one of the two Habsburg councillors thrown from the window of the Old Royal Palace in 1618, an event that came to be known as the Second Defenestration.

WENCESLAS CHAPEL

The ambulatory comes to an end at the Cathedral's chief attraction: the **Wenceslas Chapel (Svatováclavská kaple)**, which Parléř enlarged by pushing out its southern and western walls, the latter at the expense of the transept. The chapel, containing the much-restored **14th-C tomb of St Wenceslas** (d. 929 or 935), has a door of 1370 incorporating a Romanesque lion's-head knocker. Wenceslas is said to have clung to it when he was attacked and murdered by his brother Boleslav.

In homage to Charles IV's love of jewellery, the chapel is studded on its lower level with more than a thousand semi-precious stones, one of which was later thought to resemble the head of Napoleon (or someone's head—the French poet Apollinaire, on being shown this particular agate in 1902, was shocked to recognise his own features in the stone, and began fearing for his sanity). On this same level is a series of paintings of the *Passion* by an anonymous Czech artist of 1372; the story of St Wenceslas is portrayed above these, in elaborately detailed works of 1504 generally attributed to the Master of the Litoměřice Altarpiece. The room is further enhanced by Parléř's splendid ceiling, comprising parallel diagonal ribs springing from eight corbels to form a star-shaped dome.

The **Bohemian Crown Jewels** (shown to the public only on special occasions) are kept in a room above the chapel, and constitute the main survival of the extraordinary **treasury** founded by Charles IV. One of the most important cathedral treasuries in Europe, it contains numerous items that Charles brought to Prague from the court of France, and many others that were given to him as gifts by the leading dignitaries of his time; others still were commissioned from his own jewellers and goldsmiths, including the dazzling Royal Crown of Bohemia, made out of pure gold, 91 precious stones and 20 pearls. A copy of this work can be seen today in the Historical Museum at the Lobkowicz Palace (see p. 78).

CHANCEL

The long east end of the cathedral is dominated by the **Royal Mausoleum**, a large memorial in white marble executed in 1571–89 by the Dutch sculptor Alexander Collin, and surrounded by a Renaissance grille. The tombs of Bohemia's monarchs can be seen in the **Royal Crypt**, entered from the Chapel of the Holy Rood; within the crypt are also displayed the excavated remains of the cathedral's foundations, including fragments of 10th-C masonry.

BASILICA OF ST GEORGE

The Basilica of St George (Basilika sv. Jiří), founded in 905, is the oldest church in the citadel. Restoration campaigns undertaken in 1897–1907 and 1959–62 brought back many of the building's 10th-C–12th-C features, making the church one of the best-preserved Romanesque structures in Bohemia.

The main Baroque survival is the vivid ochre **west façade** (facing náměstí U sv. Jiří) and the adjoining **Chapel of St John of Nepomuk**, which is adorned on the outside with a statue of the saint. The south portal of the basilica incorporates in the tympanum a late-Gothic relief of *St George and the Dragon*, the original of which is in the National Gallery. The principal Romanesque features of the basilica's exterior are the **twin white towers** rising up at the eastern end of the church.

The cold and heavily restored interior, now deconsecrated, retains original **Romanesque arcades** in the nave. In between the two flights of the Baroque staircase that leads up to the choir is the entrance to the remarkable **crypt of 1142**, featuring columns with cubic capitals and a particularly grim and realistic sculpture of a decomposing female corpse (made in 1726).

Fragments of 16th-C painting decorate the vault of the Chapel of St Ludmila adjoining the choir. The chapel was added in the late 14th C and houses (from Petr Parléř's workshop) the **tomb of the martyred St Ludmila**, one of Bohemia's patron saints.

OLD ROYAL PALACE

HIGHLIGHTS
Vladislav Hall

An ancient seat of Bohemia's rulers, the Old Royal Palace (Starý královský palác) has parts dating back to the 12th C, but owes its present appearance largely to the rebuilding campaign undertaken by Benedikt Ried in the late 15th C. After the Habsburgs moved their quarters to the western end of the citadel, the building functioned as the central offices of the Bohemian state. It was thoroughly restored in 1924; its main rooms, which have only been open to the public since the 1960s, are still the scene of the occasional important political assembly.

The palace, entered from the castle's *Third Courtyard*, is remarkable above all for **Vladislav Hall**, architecturally one of the most exciting spaces to be seen in Europe. This vast hall—so big that jousts were once held here—was built by Benedikt Ried in 1493–1502 and is dominated by breathtaking vaulting: the ribs, likened frequently to the intertwined branches of trees, no longer play much of a structural role, but draw the visitor into the room through their powerful movements. The vaulting, an extreme development of the late-Gothic style, contrasts markedly with the innovatory Renaissance windows. Yet even when handling Classical forms, Ried is highly idiosyncratic. This can be seen in his famous door at the northeastern end of the room, where a Renaissance arch is supported by twisted pillars that seem almost a mockery of all that the Renaissance stood for.

A door in the south-west corner of the hall leads through to the former **Bohemian Chancellery**. It is famous as the place where, on May 23, 1618, a group of Protestant nobles led by Count Thurn hurled two Catholic councillors out of the window. The incident, which came to be known as the Second Defenestration, sparked off the Thirty Years War, during which the Habsburgs definitively crushed the revolt of the Bohemian nobles at the Battle of the White Mountain on the western outskirts of Prague. The north of the Vladislav Hall has a balcony, preceded by steps, overlooking the 16th C Church of All Saints (Všech Svatých), resting place of St Procopius. The extraordinary door with twisted pillars at the north-east corner of the hall leads into the **Diet Hall**, covered by another late-Gothic vault of fascinating complexity.

Through the left arch of the Renaissance double portal on the eastern side of the Vladislav Hall is a spiral staircase climbing to the rooms of the New Land Rolls; the right-hand arch leads directly to the **Riders' Staircase**, which took horses up to joust in the Vladislav Hall. Built by Ried c. 1500, the staircase again has a vault of astonishing beauty. Its ribs intersect, interrupt and are suddenly truncated. The overall effect is of suspended movement, and playful abandon shaped by rigorous geometrical discipline.

The Riders' Staircase leads down to the ground-floor rooms of Charles IV's palace, and then to the gloomy cellar below, a survival of the 12th-C palace of Prince Soběslav I. Since 2004, these Romanesque and Gothic chambers have housed a **permanent exhibition on the history of Prague Castle**, with a chronological introduction to the key events and further section dealing with particular themes, including Czech patron saints, the Church and the Cathedral, funerals and coronations, and daily life at the Castle.

GOLDEN LANE

The celebrated Golden Lane (Zlatá ulička), a row of tiny houses dating from the end of the 16th C, runs directly underneath the northeastern ramparts of the citadel, between the **White Tower** and the **Daliborka Tower**. The name of the lane is sometimes romantically associated with the alchemists at Rudolph II's court—the English clairvoyant and alchemist Edward Kelley spent two years imprisoned in the White Tower—though in fact it derives from the goldsmiths who once lived here. In the 18th and 19th centuries it was home to the very poor, and only after 1960 did the lane receive its cheerfully coloured doll's-house appearance.

The Lane's famous former residents include Franz Kafka, who rented the house at No. 22 in 1916. In the 1920s, the Nobel Prize-winning poet Jaroslav Seifert lived in a house (now gone) between the eastern end of the lane and the Daliborka Tower. The tower, another former prison, is named after the first person to be incarcerated here, the knight Dalibor of Kozojedy, whose life inspired Bedřich Smetana's opera *Dalibor* (1868).

PRAGUE CASTLE GALLERY

OPEN	April–Oct, 9 am–5 pm; Nov–March, 9 am–4 pm
CHARGES	100/50 Kč; 150 Kč family ticket
TELEPHONE	224 373 531
WEB	http://old.hrad.cz/castle/obrazarna_uk.html

MAIN ENTRANCE   Prague Castle, Second Courtyard (Prazský hrad, II. nádvorí)
METRO   Malostranská or Hradčanská
DISABLED ACCESS   Yes

HIGHLIGHTS
Titian's *Young Woman at her Toilet*
Tintoretto's *Flagellation*
Rubens' *Assembly of the Gods at Olympus*

THE BUILDING

The main rooms on the northern side of the Second Courtyard comprise the *Spanish Hall (Španělský sál)* and the *Rudolph Gallery (Rudolfova galerie)*, two mirrored and richly stuccoed halls dating back to the late 16th C but remodelled in a neo-Baroque style in 1866 for the coronation of Emperor Franz Josef I (who failed to show up at his own party and had himself crowned in Vienna instead). Generally closed to the public, the rooms are used today mainly for government meetings and receptions. The Rudolph Gallery originally housed the extraordinary art collection belonging to Emperor Rudolph II, the remnants of which can be seen in the ground-floor rooms below; these rooms, comprising what is now the Prague Castle Gallery (Obrazárna Pražského hradu), were closed for many years after a couple of visitors brazenly walked off with one of the paintings.

Rudolph II's Collection

The rule of Emperor Rudolph II (1576–1612), one of the most bizarre and colourful figures in Czech history, coincided with the last great period of court patronage in Bohemia. Rudolph's mania for art was combined with his later habit of shutting himself up in his Schatzkammer to obsessively contemplate his accumulated treasures, giving him much in common with his cousin Philip II, who shared his taste for the erotic and bizarre. His favourite sculptor was the Flemish-born Italian Mannerist

Giambologna, in whom he showed an interest that was one-sided and hardly subtle: after amassing almost all this artist's statuettes of Venus he wrote to him to ask for 'another naked female figure of the same size'. As for Rudolph's taste for the bizarre, this was amply satisfied by the Milanese artist Giuseppe Arcimboldo, whom Rudolph so admired that in 1592 he was given the title of Count Palatine. Working not only as a painter but also as an organiser of lavish festivities, Arcimboldo developed a speciality in visual punning. This was dismissed after his death as a mere curiosity but was to be greatly appreciated in the 20th C by the Surrealists: he portrayed members of the court with appropriate still-life objects, thus turning the royal gardener into a composite of flowers, and the court historiographer Wolfgang Lazius into a mass of books.

THE COLLECTION

Following Rudolph's death, most of the collection was transferred to Vienna (Arcimboldo's paintings are now in the Kunsthistorisches Museum) and what remained was plundered by the Swedes in 1648 as war booty. In the mid-17th C, Ferdinand III built up a new collection in Prague; the new gallery remained intact until 1721, when Charles IV began removing many of the better works to Vienna. Later in the century Maria Theresa sold off many more of the paintings, as did her son Joseph II in 1782. The dispersal of the collection continued throughout the 19th C, and by the end of World War I it was thought that all the paintings had gone from Prague. Investigations carried out in 1962–64 revealed that in fact many had remained in the city, and in 1965 the surviving works were brought together to form the Prague Castle Gallery. Since then, the gallery has attempted to buy back some of the original works, though there no hope of ever recreating the collection as it was in Rudolph's day.

The gallery occupies a series of newly modernised rooms, but the 120 or so works on show are largely minor ones, doing scant justice to the magnificence of the original collection. Works by

artists of Rudolph's time include Mannerist paintings by
Bartolomaeus Spranger, **Hans von Aachen** and **Cornelisz von
Harlem**. There are remarkably realistic portraits by the Bohemian
artists **Jan Kupecký** and **Petr Brandl**, including the latter's *A
Mismatched Couple at the Notary* (1700). There is also an early
painting by Rubens of the *Assembly of the Gods at Olympus*,
executed probably in Mantua in 1602.

The bulk of the collection is of the Italian 16th C and 17th C,
including a *Flagellation* and an *Adoration of the Shepherds* by
Tintoretto, a *Young Woman at her Toilet* by **Titian** (a version of a
painting in the Louvre), *St Catherine of Alexandria* and an *Angel and
Christ Washing the Feet of His Disciples* by **Veronese**, and a
peculiarly erotic *St Sebastian* by **Saraceni**, with a single arrow
placed directly in the saint's groin.

CONVENT OF ST GEORGE

OPEN	Tues–Sun, 10 am–6 pm
CHARGES	50/20 Kč; 80 Kč family ticket; free on public holidays
TELEPHONE	257 531 644. General information about the National Gallery's exhibitions: 222 321 459
WEB	www.ngprague.cz
MAIN ENTRANCE	Jiřské náměstí 33
METRO	Malostranská or Hradčanská
DISABLED ACCESS	Very limited
GUIDED VISITS	Tours in English or French are organised by the National Gallery's education department. They are 1,200 Kč for groups up to 15; 1,500 Kč for groups over 15; standard admission is also payable. To book, call 257 320 889.
SHOP	The gallery shop sells books and catalogues

HIGHLIGHTS
Karel Škréta's *Dionysio Miseroni and his Family*
Johann Georg Bendl's *St Nicholas*
Matthias Braun's *St Jude Thaddeus*
Jan Kupecký's *The Artist with his Wife*

The Convent of St George (Klášter sv. Jiří) was founded in 937 by Prince Boleslav II and his sister Princess Mlada, who became its first abbess; rebuilt several times, it was turned into a barracks after its dissolution in 1782 and then converted in 1962–72 into a branch of the National Gallery. The plain white rooms arranged around the convent's simple cloister provide a perfect setting for the Gallery's collection of 16th–18th-C Czech art, which includes a few works from the famed Rudolph collection (see p. 65).

THE COLLECTION

The collections of Mannerist and Baroque art begin on the first floor with works by artists of the Rudolph Circle, including an outstanding painting by **Bartolomaeus Spranger** of the *Risen Christ* (c. 1590), which was intended for the tomb of the artist's father-in-law, the Prague goldsmith Nicholas Müller (he appears, together with other members of his family, at the bottom of the work).

The 17th-C collections feature an especially large number of paintings by **Karel Škréta**, of which the most striking are the portraits, in particular of the French painter Nicolas Poussin (whom Škréta met in Rome in 1634–35), and an informal group portrait of the gem-carver *Dionysio Miseroni and his Family* (1653). Among the later paintings of the 17th C are the very Rubenesque *Liberation of St Andromeda* (1695) by **Michael Willmann** and a number of rapid oil sketches by **Jan Liška**, whose loosely handled and vividly coloured style is sometimes described as proto-Rococo.

Baroque sculpture is represented most notably by **Johann Georg Bendl**, who had an ability to combine Baroque drama with powerful realism—as evidenced here in his *St Nicholas* of c. 1670. Other fine sculptures include several works by **Ferdinand Brokoff**—in particular, two Moors of 1718–19 from the gates of the Mansion at Kounice and a statue of *St Ludmilla* (c. 1730)—as well as **Matthias Braun**'s hysterically posed *St Jude Thaddeus* (1712). On loan from the Carmelite Church of Our Lady of Victory in the Little Quarter (see p. 95) is a painting of the *Dream of the*

Prophet Elijah (1724) by **Petr Brandl**, one of the most successful and prolific Bohemian artists of the early 18th C: the gallery also has an extensive collection of his portraits.

A more remarkable portraitist than Bendl was **Jan Kupecký**, who is represented here by two of his greatest works, a seated portrait of the ostentatiously dressed miniaturist Karl Bruni, and a portrait of *The Artist with his Wife* (1711). The latter, a work of uncompromising realism, was painted as a token of reconciliation with his wife, who had been unfaithful and whom he portrayed here in the guise of a penitent. Of the other notable early 18th-C works, **Václav Reiner**'s *Orpheus with Animals in a Landscape* (before 1720) stands out, and there are also examples of full-blown Bohemian Rococo, such as **Antonín Kern**'s *St John on Patmos* (1737) and a cycle of miniature paintings by **Norbert Grund**.

THE CASTLE DISTRICT (HRADČANY)

The area to the west of the citadel, known as the Hradčany, suffered a devastating fire in 1541 that totally destroyed the medieval structures. However, this catastrophic event was followed by a period of intensive rebuilding which saw the district raised to the status of a royal town in 1598.

After the defeat of the Bohemian Protestants at the Battle of the White Mountain in 1620, the victorious Habsburg aristocracy filled the district with their grand palaces, most of which are beautifully preserved. This, and the almost complete absence of shops and businesses, combine to give the serene Hradčany its distinctive character—a stately architectural gem, whose enchanting streets offer welcome respite from the crowds.

ŠTERNBERG PALACE

OPEN	Tues–Sun, 10 am–6 pm
CHARGES	60/30 Kč; 90 Kč family ticket
TELEPHONE	220 514 634-7. General information about the National Gallery's exhibitions: 222 321 459
WEB	www.ngprague.cz
MAIN ENTRANCE	Hradčanské náměstí 15
METRO	Malostranská, then tram 22
DISABLED ACCESS	No
GUIDED VISITS	Tours in English or French are organised by the National Gallery's education department: 1,200 Kč for groups up to 15; 1,500 Kč for groups over 15 ; standard admission also payable. To book call 220 51 45 98.
SHOP	Gallery shop sells books and catalogues.
EAT	Café Galerie in the courtyard

HIGHLIGHTS

Hans Süss of Kulmbach's *panels showing Emperor Henry II and Empress Kunegunda*

Albrecht Dürer's *The Feast of the Rosary*

Jan Gossaert's *St Luke Drawing the Virgin and Child*

Simon Vouet's *Suicide of Lucretia*

Rubens' *Portrait of the Marchese Ambrogio Spinola*

Rembrandt's *Scholar in his Study*

THE BUILDING

Built between 1698 and 1707, the Šternberg Palace (Šternberský palác) is a gloomy but impressive structure completely hidden from Hradčany Square. The building is particularly remarkable for its courtyard, dominated on its western side by a large oval pavilion, and for the rooms themselves, which feature a number of fine 18th-C stuccoed and painted ceilings. These rooms provide a suitably elegant setting for the pre-modern Foreign School holdings of the National Gallery, which have been housed here since 1945 (the modern works are now displayed in the Trade Fair

ŠTERNBERG PALACE

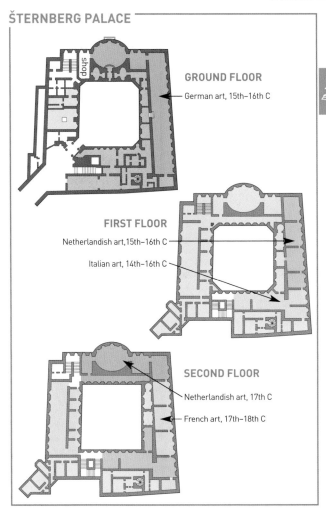

GROUND FLOOR

German art, 15th–16th C

FIRST FLOOR

Netherlandish art, 15th–16th C

Italian art, 14th–16th C

SECOND FLOOR

Netherlandish art, 17th C

French art, 17th–18th C

shop

Albrecht Dürer *The Feast of the Rosary* (1506)

Palace in Holešovice; see p. 131). Although the collection has been broken up in recent years, with many paintings returned to their pre-war owners and to the Church, the gallery still contains several masterpieces that more than justify a visit. The main staircase adjoining the ticket office leads up to the first and second floors where the bulk of the collection is shown; the ground floor section is entered from the courtyard.

THE COLLECTION
GROUND FLOOR

The true quality of the gallery is felt in the excellent group of *German 15th–16th-C paintings* displayed here. These include a massive altarpiece by **Hans Raphon** comprising 13 Passion scenes (c. 1499); **Hans Schücklin**'s *Beheading of St Barbara* (1470); monochrome fragments of an altarpiece of 1509 by **Hans Holbein** the Elder and a portrait by his son; and **Baldung Grien**'s *Decapitation of St Dorothy* (1516). There are a variety of works by **Lucas Cranach the Elder**, most notably a delightful *Adam and Eve* of 1537 and a portrait entitled *The Old Fool* of c. 1530, in which a girl picks an old man's pocket. Especially powerful are two large panels by **Hans Süss of Kulmbach**, vigorous and near-life-sized representations of the Emperor Henry II and the Empress Kunegunda.

Süss was an artist greatly influenced by **Albrecht Dürer**, who is represented here by one of his most famous works, *The Feast of the Rosary* (see opposite page). Painted in Venice in 1506 for the church of San Bartolomeo (the church of Venice's merchant colony), this work shows the great influence on the artist of the brilliant colouring of Venetian painters such as Giovanni Bellini. In turn, the painting made an enormous impact on the Venetian public, and indeed was their first main contact with contemporary German art. Among the many contemporary personalities that Dürer vividly portrayed on either side of the enthroned Virgin are Pope Julius II, Emperor Maximilian I, Domenico Grimani, Jakob Fugger and Hieronymus of Augsburg. The artist himself, a man not known for his modesty, also included a self-portrait among this distinguished company (he is standing under a tree, holding his signature). The painting was acquired by Rudolph II in 1606, and is the most important of his pictures to have remained in Prague.

FIRST FLOOR

The *14th–16th-C Italian paintings* on display here include an expressive *Lamentation* by **Lorenzo di Monaco**; of the holdings of art from the Netherlands of the 15th and 16th centuries, **Jan Gossaert**'s monumental *St Luke Drawing the Virgin and Child* (1513–16) and **Pieter Brueghel the Elder**'s *Haymaking* (1565) stand out. The former was hung on the main altar of St Vitus's Cathedral from 1618 up to the end of the 19th C, while the latter formed part of a famous series of panels of the months (the other surviving panels from this series are in the Kunsthistorisches Museum in Vienna).

SECOND FLOOR

This begins with the small and unimpressive holdings of *17th- and 18th-C French paintings*. The best of the paintings—a dramatically coloured *Suicide of Lucretia* (1625/6) by **Simon Vouet**—was painted in Rome under the influence of Caravaggio and is thus displayed in the rooms devoted to the 17th- and 18th-C Italian School.

The *Netherlandish 17th-C holdings* are extensive and feature genre scenes, still lifes and landscapes. The two outstanding works in this section are **Rembrandt**'s *Scholar in his Study* (1634) and the half-length portrait by **Frans Hals** of *Jasper Schade van Westrum* (c. 1645).

SANCTUARY OF OUR LADY OF LORETO

OPEN	Tues–Sun, 9 am–12.15 and 1 pm–4.30 pm
CHARGES	80/60 Kč
TELEPHONE	220 516 740
MAIN ENTRANCE	Loretánské náměstí 7
METRO	Malostranská, then tram 22
RELIGIOUS SERVICES	Saturday 7.30 am (Virgin's House), Sunday 6 pm (Church of the Nativity)
DISABLED ACCESS	Limited
SHOP	On-site shop sells books and souvenirs
EAT	Try U Ševce Matouše (see p. 82) and U Černého vola on Loretánské náměstí

HIGHLIGHTS
Virgin's House
17th-C Diamond Monstrance

The sanctuary dates back to 1626, when Benigna Kateřina of Lobkowicz, anxious to revive the Marian cult, commissioned a replica of the Santa Casa, or Virgin's House, of the Italian town of Loreto. According to a 15th-C tradition, the house was transported to Loreto miraculously from the Holy Land. At least

50 other copies of this house have been made, but the one in Prague remains the most famous. The Virgin's House is encased in a Baroque complex, the main, western façade of which was begun by Christoph Dientzenhofer in 1716 and completed by his son Kilian Ignaz in 1722. The elegant façade has a tall tower enclosing an elaborate carillon of 1694, which plays various melodies, including—at the stroke of every hour—the Marian hymn 'We Greet Thee a Thousand Times'. Each year crowds of Catholic pilgrims come to pray at this holy shrine.

INTERIOR

The **Virgin's House** (1626-31) stands in the middle of the cloisters, shrouded in rich stucco decoration featuring Old Testament figures and scenes from the Life of the Virgin. The simple interior contains a polychrome figure of the Virgin and Child, set in a striking silver niche. The **cloisters** themselves date back to 1661 but were raised one storey by K.I. Dientzenhofer in the 1740s. They are surrounded by small and elaborately decorated 18th-C chapels containing wooden altars and confessionals; the corner chapel to the right of the main entrance contains an extraordinary **sculpture of the bearded St Wilgefortis**, the patron of unhappily married women.

   The **treasury**, situated off the western side of the cloisters, contains chalices, monstrances and other liturgical objects. Among these is the famous **Diamond Monstrance** (known also as 'the Prague Sun'), which was designed by the great Viennese architect Johann Bernhard Fischer von Erlach in the 1690s. A gift from Ludmila Eva Franziska (who donated her entire estate to the sanctuary), it is made of 12 kg of silver gilt and uses 6,222 of the 6,500 diamonds sewn onto her wedding dress (the rest comprised the craftsmen's fee). One of the more delightful touches of this spectacular piece of fantasy is the tiny enamel dove floating serenely within the explosion of rays.

STRAHOV MONASTERY

OPEN	**Library halls** Daily, 9 am–12 pm and 1 pm–5 pm **Strahov art gallery** Tues–Sun, 9 am–12 pm and 12.30 pm–5 pm
CHARGES	**Library halls** 70/50 Kč **Strahov art gallery** 40/2o Kč
TELEPHONE	220 516 671
WEB	www.strahovskyklaster.cz
MAIN ENTRANCE	Strahovské nádvoří 1
METRO	Malostranská, then tram 22
DISABLED ACCESS	Limited
SHOP	On-site bookshop (first floor)
EAT	Restaurace Peklo (see p. 81) is situated inside the monastery complex.

HIGHLIGHTS
Philosophical Hall
Theological Hall
9th-C Strahov New Testament

The Premonstratensian Monastery of Strahov was founded by Vladislav II in 1140 and, with its formidable library, soon became one of the great centres of learning in Bohemia. Devastated and plundered by the Swedes in 1648, the place prospered once again after the Treaty of Westphalia, and acquired so many books that in 1671 a new library hall was built (known today as the Theological Hall). Towards the end of the following century a further library hall, the Philosophical Hall, was built.

Since 1989, monks have once again occupied the monastery and have vigorously set about making the complex more commercially viable: the monastery's brewing traditions have been revived, several of its buildings have been profitably leased out (such as the 17th-C Church of St Roch—now the Galerie Miró, see p. 80), and the place's tourist potential has been exploited to the full.

LIBRARY HALLS

The finest of the Baroque additions to the monastery are its two library halls, entered adjacent to the 12th-C Monastery Church of Our Lady. The first and grander of the two, the **Philosophical Hall**, was built at the end of the 18th C around richly gilded and carved walnut furnishings brought here from a dissolved Premonstratensian monastery. In 1794, one of the greatest fresco painters of Central Europe, the Austrian Franz Maulbertsch, covered the entire vault of this hall with a superb ceiling painting representing the theme of *The Struggle of Mankind to Know True Wisdom*.

The **Theological Hall** has kept its original wooden shelving and 17th and 18th-C globes. Tables display a select few of the library's unique collection of illuminated manuscripts and incunabula. Among these is the Strahov New Testament, an Ottonian work of the 9th–10th C and one of the oldest written documents in the Czech Republic (it is displayed just outside the hall). The magnificent ceiling of the Theological Hall is decorated with late-17th-C stucco cartouches framing frescoes celebrating human knowledge.

STRAHOV ART GALLERY

This small but worthwhile gallery situated on the upper floor of the monastery cloisters features some of the works of art acquired by the monks over the centuries, returned to them by the post-Communist government. The collection, an eclectic mix of religious art, portraits, landscapes, still lifes and sculpture, is chaotically arranged and without any particular division into themes or periods. It ranges from an excellent small group of medieval paintings—including the chubbily featured mid-14th-C *Strahov Madonna* and some marvellously realistic late-15th-C works attributed to the **Master of Litoměřice**—to a number of fine Baroque and Rococo oils by **Karel Škréta**, **Petr Brandl**, **Sebastiano Ricci**, **Antonín Kern** and **Franz Maulbertsch**.

in the area

PRAGUE CASTLE

Powder Tower (Mihulka) Vikářská, Prague Castle. Open daily.
April–Oct, 9 am–5 pm; Nov–March, 9 am–4 pm. 224 373 368, 224
372 434-5, www.hrad.cz. This round medieval tower guards the
castle's northern bastions, which were rebuilt by Benedikt Ried in
1485. Its two floors contain an exhibition, in Czech only, on
Renaissance life at the castle. *M* to Malostranská or Hradčanská
Map p. 51, 1B

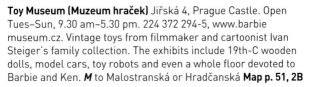

Toy Museum (Muzeum hraček) Jiřská 4, Prague Castle. Open
Tues–Sun, 9.30 am–5.30 pm. 224 372 294-5, www.barbie
museum.cz. Vintage toys from filmmaker and cartoonist Ivan
Steiger's family collection. The exhibits include 19th-C wooden
dolls, model cars, toy robots and even a whole floor devoted to
Barbie and Ken. *M* to Malostranská or Hradčanská **Map p. 51, 2B**

Historical Museum, Lobkowicz Palace (Lobkovický palác) Jiřská 3,
Prague Castle. Open Tues–Sun, 9 am–5 pm. 257 535 121. An
exhibition run by the National Museum documenting the history of
Bohemia from the arrival of the Slavs up to 1848–49. More
interesting than the display is the palace itself, which was rebuilt
in 1651–68 and retains several original ceilings, including (in
Room 19) a heavily stuccoed 17th-C ceiling incorporating an
amusing painted panel of the *Triumph of Caesar*. *M* to
Malostranská or Hradčanská **Map p. 51, 2B**

Prague Castle Riding School (Jízdárna Pražského hradu) U
Prašného mostu 55, Prague Castle. Open 10 am–6 pm. 224 371
111, www.hrad.cz. This elegantly simple Baroque building in the
castle grounds was designed by Jean-Baptiste Mathey in 1694 as
a royal riding school. Restored in the 1950s, it is now used for
temporary art exhibitions. *M* to Malostranská or Hradčanská **Map
p. 50, 4A**

Ball-Game Court (Míčovna) Královská zahrada, Prague Castle. 224
373 368, 224 372 434-5, www.hrad.cz. Set in the beautifully

maintained and azalea-laden Royal Gardens, this harmonious Renaissance structure was built by Bonifác Wohlmut and Ulrico Avostalis in 1565–69. It is covered all over with much-restored, though still impressive, Renaissance *sgrafitto* work. The interior is used for concerts and art exhibitions. *M* to Malostranská or Hradčanská **Map p. 51, 1A**

Summer Palace (Letohrádek královny Anny) Královská zahrada, Prague Castle. Open May–Oct, Tues–Sun, 10 am–6 pm. 224 373 368, 224 372 434-5, www.hrad.cz. Popularly known as the Belvedere, this building is one of the purest examples in Central Europe of the Italian Renaissance style, the proportions of its arcaded lower level strongly recalling the architecture of Brunelleschi. It was completed in 1552–69 by Bonifác Wohlmut, who provided it with the one feature that reveals it as a work situated in Central Europe rather than Italy—the curious copper roof shaped like the inverted hull of a ship. Exquisite mythological and ornamental reliefs by Paolo della Stella adorn the arcade; the interior, used for art exhibitions, was remodelled in the mid-19th C and restored after World War II. *M* to Malostranská or Hradčanská **Map p. 51, 2A**

CASTLE DISTRICT (HRADČANY)

Nový Svět Street (New World) One of Prague's most picturesque streets—a quiet cobbled lane lined with small 16th-C terraced houses. No. 1, on the left-hand side, belonged first to Tycho Brahe and then, after 1600, to his successor as court astronomer, Johannes Kepler; the two men are commemorated by a plaque. By the 19th-C the houses had fallen into disrepair and were inhabited by the very poor, but they are now some of Prague's most exclusive addresses. *M* to Malostranská, then tram 22 **Map p. 50, 2B**

Černín Palace (Černínský palác) Loretánské náměstí. This vast Baroque building, occupying the entire western side of Loreto Square, was designed in 1669 for the imperial ambassador to Venice. The palace was extensively restored and remodelled in 1928–34, but the monumental façade overlooking the square remains, in conception if not in detailing, essentially as planned. Since 1918, the building has housed the Ministry of Foreign Affairs. It was the scene of a notorious incident in 1948, when the last non-Communist member of the government, Jan Masaryk (the son of Czechoslovakia's first president), fell out of one of the windows and died. Though the official verdict was suicide, the incident became the subject of intense speculation. *M* to Malostranská, then tram 22 **Map p. 50, 2B-C**

Museum of Miniatures (Muzeum miniatur) Strahovské nádvoří 10. Open daily, 9 am–5 pm. 233 352 371. A collection of weird and fascinating miniatures painstakingly created by the Russian artist Anatoly Konenko, who is in the *Guinness Book of Records* for producing the world's smallest book. The exhibits—which include a portrait of Anton Chekhov on half a poppyseed, a train on a strand of hair, and a camel caravan in the eye of a needle—are so tiny that they can only be viewed through a microscope or magnifying glass. *M* to Malostranská, then tram 22 **Map p. 50, 2C**

commercial galleries

Galerie Miró Strahovské nádvoří 1, 233 354 066. Open Tue–Sun, 10 am–5 pm. The gallery, located inside a deconsecrated 17th-C church within the peaceful confines of the Strahov Monastery (see p. 76), sells contemporary Czech art as well as original (albeit minor) works by famous foreign artists, such as Picasso, Miró, Dalí, Braque, Rouault and Chagall. *M* to Malostranská, then tram No. 22 **Map p. 50, 2C**

Gambra Černínská 5, 220 514 527, www.illumin.co.uk/svank/misc/gambra.html. Open Mar–Oct, Wed–Sun, 12 pm–6 pm; Nov–Feb, Sat–Sun, 12 pm–5.30 pm. A small gallery owned by the celebrated animator Jan Švankmajer and his wife Eva. The exhibits comprise a cluttered and fascinating collection of collages, ceramics and lithographs by the Švankmajers, Karel Baron, and other prominent members of the Czech surrealist movement, which has been active in Prague since the 1920s. *M* to Malostranská, then tram No. 22 **Map p. 50, 2B**

Josef Sudek Gallery Úvoz 24, 257 531 489. Open Wed–Sun, 11 am–7 pm. Josef Sudek, widely seen as the father of modern Czech photography, concentrated on the abstract qualities of everyday scenes and objects, and also created some of the most evocative images ever produced of Prague. The gallery, located in the flat where Sudek lived from 1959 until his death in 1976, puts on regular exhibitions that chart the development of photography in the 20th C. *M* to Malostranská **Map p. 50, 3C**

eat

AT THE MUSEUMS

€   **Café Galerie** Hradčanské náměstí 15. This pleasant café is in the courtyard of the Šternberg Palace. It serves refreshments and light snacks. *M* to Malostranská or Hradčanská **Map p. 50, 4B**

Restaurace v zahradě "Na Baště" (Café Poet) Pražský hrad, 224 373 599. Set in a small garden to the left of the main entrance to Prague Castle, this is a convenient place to stop for breakfast or lunch before touring the citadel. *M* to Malostranská or Hradčanská **Map p. 51, 2B**

€€€ **Restaurace Peklo** Strahovské nádvoří 1, 220 516652. This upmarket restaurant (amusingly, the name translates as 'Hell') is within the Strahov Monastery complex. The premises have been converted from medieval wine cellar, so ventilation can be a problem. The menu is Czech and international cuisine. *M* to Malostranská, then tram 22 **Map p. 50, 2C**

SURROUNDING AREA

€€   **Faros** Šporková 5. 257 533 964. For a quiet lunch or dinner in the Castle District, try this Greek restaurant not far from Malostranské náměstí. Succulent lamb chops and a fresh array of Greek meze served in a rustic tavern take you worlds away from cabbage. *M* to Malostranská **Map p. 50, 4C**

U Ševce Matouše Loretánské náměstí, 220 514 536. This site was a former shoemaker's, and is under the arcades on Loreto Square. It's convenient if you've been visiting the Loreto shrine (see p. 74). The restaurant serves traditional Czech cuisine. *M* to Malostranská or Hradčanská **Map p. 50, 2C**

€€€ **U Zlaté hrušky** Nový svět 3, 220 514 778. An intimate 'cellar style' restaurant, U Zlaté Hrušky is located in a small house on one of Prague's most picturesque streets. The notice outside cheerfully advises patrons about the choice available: 'Specialities from the Czech duck' and 'For the guests who are not able to eat a Czech duck'. *M* to Malostranská or Hradčanská **Map p. 50, 2B**

shop

MISCELLANEOUS

Pavla & Olga Vlašská 13, 257 532 851. This small atelier on the route up to the castle sells hand-woven fabrics, including heavy wools and gorgeous silks. The clothes in the shop are just samples; the designers can make anything to order. *M* to Malostranská **Map p. 51, 1C**

Porcelain House Úvoz 1, 257 532 726. This small shop sells finely detailed miniature porcelain houses modelled on Prague buildings. The owners will ship products abroad on request. *M* to Malostranská **Map p. 50, 4C**

Hračky Pohořelec 24, 22, 359, 127. This store, just a short walk from the castle, has an excellent selection of wonderful Czech-made tin toys. It's worth browsing, even if you're not in the market. *M* to Hradčanská **Map p. 50, 2C**

THE LITTLE QUARTER (MALÁ STRANA)

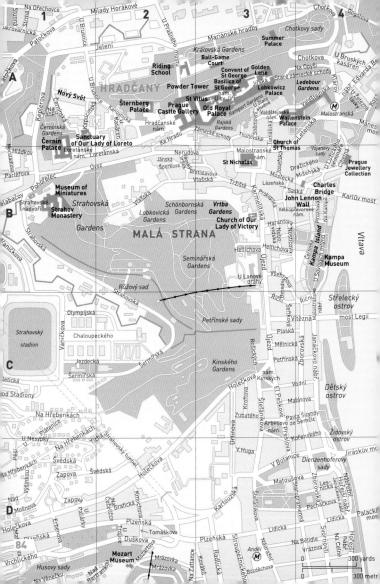

The Little Quarter, or Malá Strana, is a surprisingly compact area, delineated by the Hradčany to the north-west and the Vltava river to the east. It is in many ways Prague's most appealing district—a labyrinth of charming cobbled backstreets that have so far escaped the worst of the commercialisation affecting the Old Town. These streets have changed so little since the 18th-C that they almost appear as a giant, fantastical film-set, and indeed have been used as such. Shops and businesses cluster around Malá Strana's main thoroughfare, Nerudova, which forms part of the coronation route once used by Czech kings (now throngs of tourists make the daily ascent up to the Castle).

Yet, away from Nerudova, Malá Strana is mainly residential. The former Gothic town, founded here in 1257 by King Přemysl Otakar II, was entirely wiped away by a devastating fire in 1541. In its place rose imposing Baroque palaces, put up by the Habsburg nobility after 1648. Attached to these palaces are beautiful terraced gardens, some of which are open to the public—most notably the so-called 'Gardens Below Prague Castle' laid out in 1716 by the Italian architect Santini-Aichel. Unlike the flat Staré Město, Malá Strana is steeply pitched, and incorporates Petřín Hill, a large wooded park with panoramic views of the city that is ideal for afternoon walks.

Little Quarter square (Malostranské náměstí) surrounded today by buildings of largely 17th- and 18th-C appearance, was for centuries the site of a market and town hall, and to this day remains the commercial centre of the district.

Church of St Nicholas

OPEN	**Church** 9 am–4.45 pm daily **Belfry** 10 am–6 pm daily
CHARGES	50/25 Kč; free for services
TELEPHONE	257 534 215
MAIN ENTRANCE	Malostranské náměstí 38
METRO	Malostranská
DISABLED ACCESS	Yes
EAT	There are plenty of restaurants and cafés on the Little Quarter Square.

HIGHLIGHTS
18th-C statues by Ignác Platzer the Elder
18th-C *Apotheosis of St Nicholas*
17th-C altarpiece of the Holy Rood

The Church of St Nicholas (sv. Mikuláš) in the Little Quarter—not to be confused with its Old Town namesake—is one of the outstanding Baroque buildings of Central Europe, rivalled only by Prague Castle as the dominant element in the city's skyline. Commissioned by the Jesuits, whose college stands nearby, the church was begun in 1703 under the direction of Christoph Dientzenhofer. The west façade and nave were completed by 1711, but work was temporarily halted due to financial difficulties, only to be resumed after 1737 by Dientzenhofer's son, Kilian Ignaz. Despite its protracted construction, the church of St Nicholas has an impressive unity, and its undulating west façade, with its remarkably rich play of concave and convex surfaces, is one of the great architectural delights of Prague.

A truly astonishing array of golds, pinks and pastel greens is the most immediately striking feature of the interior. The nave walls, with their curved balconies and giant, obliquely set pilasters, exude an extraordinary sense of movement, and create a flowing line that culminates in the enormous oval of the crossing.

The nave vaulting, with its intersecting ribs, is obscured by a vast ceiling painting by Johann Lukas Kracker, *The Apotheosis of St Nicholas* (1760–61). The dome, meanwhile, is covered by *The Celebration of the Holy Trinity* (1752–53) by Franz Palko, who also did many of the wall-paintings in the chancel.

More impressive still is the magnificent statuary, particularly the agitated saints along the nave, the four figures of the Church Fathers in the corners of the crossing, and the statue of St Nicholas at the High Altar—all the work of **Ignác Platzer the Elder**.

Wallenstein Palace & Gardens

OPEN	**Palace** (by guided tour only) Sat and Sun, 10 am–5 pm
	Gardens Apr–Oct, 10 am–6 pm daily
	Riding School Tues–Sun, 10 am–6 pm
CHARGES	**Palace** and **Gardens** Free admission
	Riding School Varies according to exhibition
TELEPHONE	**Palace** (upper house of the Czech Parliament) 257 071 111
	Gardens 257 072 759
	Riding School 257 073 136
WEB	**Riding School** www.ngprague.cz
MAIN ENTRANCE	**Palace** and **Gardens** Valdštejnské náměstí 4
	Riding School Valdštejnská 3
METRO	Malostranská
DISABLED ACCESS	Yes
EAT	There are restaurants and cafés on Malostranské náměstí.

HIGHLIGHTS
17th-C fresco of Albrecht of Wallenstein
17th-C sala terrena
17th-C sculpture of Hercules

Relaxing in the Wallenstein Gardens

THE BUILDING

The narrow Valdštejnské náměstí is named after the Wallenstein Palace on its eastern side, built in 1623–30 for the great Albrecht of Wallenstein, whose family seat it was until 1945. Wallenstein, a Habsburg general renowned as much for his military genius as for his avarice, deceitfulness and megalomania, was one of the most colourful figures in Czech history. His mercurial career and inevitably tragic end have inspired numerous writers, most notably Schiller, whose *Wallenstein* is one of the outstanding works of German Romantic drama. Wallenstein's suitably imposing palace was the earliest of the many grand palaces erected in Prague in the 17th and 18th centuries. Its interior, now home to the upper house of the Czech Parliament, features a splendid main hall. The stuccoed ceiling incorporates a fresco representing Wallenstein himself dressed as Mars and riding in a chariot; the work was executed in 1630, only four years before Wallenstein's ignominious murder after years of political and military scheming.

THE GARDENS

The Wallenstein Gardens (Valdštejnská zahrada), laid out in the early 17th C, are a perfect spot to escape the crowds and noise of the city. Architecturally, their most impressive structure is the tall and magnificent loggia, or sala terrena. The loggia overlooks the gardens' central avenue, which is lined with bronze statues copied after works by Adriaen de Vries, the originals having been looted by the Swedes in 1648 (they now stand outside the Swedish Royal Palace at Drottningholm).

To the right of the loggia, parallel to Letenská, is an aviary with peacocks—for which the gardens were once famous—and a curious 'stalactite wall' that seems very out of place in the verdant surroundings. The central avenue leads northeast via fountains to a large fishpond adorned with a bronze sculpture of Hercules, an original by de Vries. Overlooking the pond is the former Wallenstein Riding School, now used for temporary exhibitions put on by the National Gallery. The entrance is on the other side of the building, by the elegant Malostranská metro station (1978) with its small forecourt, café and fountains.

Gardens Below Prague Castle

OPEN	Apr–Oct, 10 am–6 pm daily
CHARGES	95/40 Kč
TELEPHONE	257 010 401
WEB	www.prazskezahrady.cz/en/pz.html
ENTRANCES	**Ledebour Palace** Valdštejnská náměstí 4
	Pálffy Palace Valdštejnská 12–14
	Rampart Garden Prague Castle Zahrada na Valech
METRO	Malostranská

DISABLED ACCESS   Only the parterre of the Ledebour Palace garden
EAT   There are restaurants and cafés on Malostranské náměstí.

HIGHLIGHTS

18th-C gardens of the Ledebour Palace
Views from the terrace of the early-18th-C Pálffy Palace
18th-C gardens of the Kolowrat Palace

The wonderful terraced gardens of the palaces along
Valdštejnská were restored during the 1990s thanks to help from
the Prague Heritage Fund, and today form part of a public park
known as the Gardens Below Prague Castle (Zahrady pod
Pražským hradem). The first of the palaces—the Ledebour Palace
(Ledeburský palác)—is situated in the northwestern corner of
Valdštejnské náměstí, and is a late-Baroque structure designed
by Ignác Jan Palliardi in 1787. Its beautiful gardens rise steeply
from a richly stuccoed *sala terrena* (today used for concerts) up to
a belvedere, the whole enlivened by fountains and a statue of
Hercules. The adjoining early-18c Pálffy Palace (Pálffy palác) is
now a music academy that also houses one of Prague's most
atmospheric restaurants (see p. 98), with views onto the Pálffy
gardens.

   The Kolowrat Palace (Kolowratský palác) was designed by
Palliardi in 1784. He was also responsible for laying out its
gardens, which are perhaps the finest of them all, comprising a
luxuriant Rococo complex of staircases, terraces, fountains,
loggias, balustrades and pools. The last of the great palaces along
Valdštejnská is the Fürstenberg Palace, built in 1743–47 by an
unknown architect clearly influenced by K.I. Dientzenhofer; it is
now the Polish Embassy, and the renewal of its attractive 18th-C
gardens is being planned.

Kampa Museum

Kampa Museum

OPEN	Open daily, 10 am–6 pm
CHARGES	95/40 Kč
TELEPHONE	257 286 147
WEB	www.museumkampa.cz
ENTRANCES	U Sovových mlýnů 2
METRO	Malostranská

HIGHLIGHTS
František Kupka's *Cathedral*
Otto Gutfreund's *Viki*
Jiří Kolář's *Apple*

Karel Malich *Landscape with Eternity* (1980–1983)

The museum—occupying a converted 14th-C mill in the southern half of Kampa Island—is the brainchild of the Washington-based Jan and Meda Mládek, who personally amassed the collection over several decades despite often being barred from Czechoslovakia. The exhibition includes a permanent display of works by František Kupka (whom Meda Mládek knew from her student days in Paris), Otto Gutfreund and Jiří Kolář. There are also works by other Central European artists of the 1960s and 1970s. The museum has now reopened following the devastating floods of 2002; in a particularly dramatic incident, a giant sculpture that stood in front of the museum was washed almost 45 kilometres downriver.

THE COLLECTION

Because of the personal relationship between the Mládeks and **František Kupka**, the museum has a particularly good collection of the artist's colourful works. Kupka was born in 1871 in eastern Bohemia, and studied in Prague and later Vienna. Although he began with heroic, patriotic concepts, he turned from figure drawing to abstract art around the turn of the century, and early works on display such as the studies he did for paintings like *Newton's Circles* (1911–1912) trace this development. Kupka was also well-known as an illustrator and designer, and the museum has examples of his studies for everything from book illustrations to carpet patterns. The artist eventually settled in Paris, in 1896, where he founded, with Jean Arp, the group known as Abstraction-Création.

Otto Gutfreund is another focus of the museum. Born in Prague in 1889, he was one of the leading Cubist sculptors of his day. Like so many others of his generation, he spent time in France, also studying under Bourdelle, but returned to Prague to continue working. Here he joined the Group of Plastic Artists, artists that mixed Cubism and Expressionism. The Kampa Museum has 17 Gutfreund sculptures, a significant amount of the artist's output.

The **Jiří Kolář** collection includes a wide range of this experimental collage-maker's work. A dissident throughout his life, Kolář emigrated in 1979 to Paris, where he lived until his death in 2002. He is best known for his innovative creative techniques, ranging from *crumplage*—where images are crumpled and pasted on paper—to *prolage*—combining images within textured three dimensions—to *chiasmage*—covering an object with letters, text and notation.

The museum also has a collection of various Central European art, mostly from the 1960s and 1970s.

in the area

Church of St Thomas Josefská 8. Attached to an Augustinian friary with a beautiful inner courtyard, this medieval church was remodelled in 1722–31 by K.I. Dientzenhofer, who gave the main façade a dramatic appearance through the addition of massive, projecting forms. *M* to Malostranská **Map p. 84, 3A**

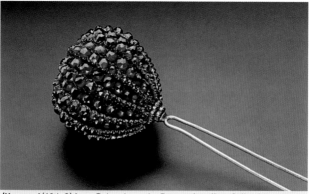

'**Harpoon**' (19th C) from Bohemia, at the Prague Jewellery Collection

Prague Jewellery Collection (Pražský kabinet šperku) Cihelná 2b.
Open daily 10 am–6 pm. 221 451 400. A small, recently opened
museum situated by the riverside, with a display of jewellery,
goldwork and luxury decorative items dating from the 17th C
onwards. The collections belong to the Museum of Decorative
Arts. *M* to Malostranská **Map p. 84, 4B**

John Lennon Wall (Lennonova zeď) Velkopřevorské náměstí.
Following John Lennon's death in 1980, the garden wall of the
Grand Prior's Palace was spray-painted with graffiti in an
improvised, multi-coloured homage to the Beatle. The
Communist authorities, and later the Knights of Malta (who
reclaimed the building in 1990), made several attempts to remove
the graffiti, but eventually gave up in the face of public opposition.
The wall has now become something of a Prague landmark,
though the current mess of scribblings (mostly done by tourists)
bears little relation to Lennon or his life. *M* to Malostranská **Map
p. 84, 4B**

Kampa Island One of the most beautiful areas of Prague,
separated from the west bank of the Vltava by the Čertovka, or
'Devil's Stream'. Until the late 16th C, the island was entirely
vineyards, gardens and fields. Most of the houses on this 'Venice
of Prague' overlook the quiet and tree-lined Na Kampě, which
broadens into a picturesque square just below the Charles
Bridge. Kampa Island is host to several good places to eat and
drink, including the superb Kampa Park (see p. 100), with
fantastic views from its riverside terrace. *M* to Malostranská **Map
p. 84, 4B**

Carmelite Church of Our Lady of Victory (Panny Marie vítězné)
Karmelitská 9. Open daily, 9.30 am–5.30 pm. 257 533 646. This
former Lutheran church, rebuilt by the Carmelites in 1624, is one
of the many dreary European imitations of the Gesù in Rome. The
rather plain interior, however, is much visited on account of a tiny
16th-C votive image of the Infant Christ—the so-called Bambino di
Praga—displayed in a chapel on the right of the nave (see picture
on p. 96). The Carmelite nuns have taken pains to exploit the full
commercial potential of this ecclesiastical Barbie doll, regularly

changing its outfits for the benefit of tourists; some of these outfits are displayed in the small upstairs museum, where there is also video show of the famed Bambino. Of greater artistic interest than the image itself is the gilded wooden altar on which it has been placed, a Rococo structure carved in 1776. *M* to Malostranská **Map p. 84, 3B**

The 'Infant of Prague'

Mozart Museum Mozartova 169 (Bertramka). Open Apr–Oct, Tues–Sun, 9.30–6 pm; Nov–Mar, 9.30 am–5 pm. 257 318 461. This recently restored 18th-C villa, with a wooden gallery and quiet, leafy garden, was the late-18th-C home of the composer František Xaver Dušek and his wife Josefa, a famous singer. The couple were close friends of Mozart, who stayed with them in 1786, 1787 and 1791. Their house has now been done up as a delightful Mozart Museum, with appropriate furnishings, unobtrusive background music, and several mementoes of the composer's stay in Prague, including a piano and harpsichord on which he allegedly played. Recitals are held here (see p. 152). *M* to Anděl **Map p. 84, 2D**

Mozart in Prague

It is perhaps thanks above all to Mozart that the Czechs today are so famed internationally as a music-loving nation. The great composer came to the city in 1787 to attend the production of his *Marriage of Figaro*, a work that had been coldly received in Vienna but whose success in Prague amounted, in the words of his biographer, 'to absolute intoxication and frenzy'. Mozart was certainly exhilarated by this reaction, and his love affair with the city continued throughout his life. Two of his greatest works—the *Prague Symphony* and the opera *Don Giovanni*—were composed here, the latter dedicated to the 'good people of Prague'. With his health failing, Mozart returned to Prague in 1791 to compose an opera—*La Clemenza di Tito*—for the coronation of the Emperor Leopold. When the composer died in Vienna later in the year, the inhabitants of Prague mourned his death in spectacular fashion and have maintained an enormous affection for him ever since. He has come to be treated not only as an honorary Czech, but also as a person integral to the stereotypical image of the city—a status enormously enhanced by the filming here in 1984 of Czech director Miloš Forman's film *Amadeus*.

commercial galleries

Antikva Nova Kodl Vítězná 11, 251 512 728, www.galeriekodl.cz. Open Mon–Fri, 10 am–1 pm and 2 pm–6 pm. An auction house and gallery specialising in 19th-C and 20th-C Czech art; Emil Filla's *Poissons d'or vers une fenêtre* was sold here in 2000 for a whopping 7.2 million Kč. The gallery has a huge exhibition space and also deals in antique jewellery, glass, porcelain and furniture. *M* to Národní třída **Map p. 84, 4C**

Galerie MXM Nosticova 6, 257 311 198. Open Tues–Sun, 11.30 am–6 pm. The oldest private gallery in Prague (founded in 1990; hence the name), MXM is still very influential despite its modest exhibition space—a single vaulted room stuck away in a tatty courtyard. The shows are always of a high standard, and this is one of the best places to buy works by up-and-coming Czech artists such as Petr Písařík, Michal Gabriel and Tomáš Hlavina. *M* to Malostranská **Map p. 84, 3B**

Josef Sudek's Studio Újezd 30, 251 510 760, www.sudek-atelier.cz. Open Tues–Sun, 12 pm–6 pm. The studio where Sudek worked for many decades was completely renovated in 2000 and is now open to the public. On display are photographs by young Czech artists as well as some of Sudek's own fascinating work. *M* to Malostranská **Map p. 84, 3B**

eat

Some of the city's best restaurants are found in this district of Prague, many taking advantage of riverside locations near Kampa Island. This area west of the Vltava, set beneath the castle, feels very much like a village far from Prague's bustling Old Town.

RESTAURANTS

€ **Bar Bar** Všehrdova 17, 257 312 246. This cosy basement bar doubles as a crêperie. It's ideal for quick snacks, although a bit off the beaten track. *M* to Malostranská **Map p. 84, 3B**

Malostranská kavárna Malostranské náměstí (Grömling Palace). A smartly refurbished café with a long history behind it, situated in the middle of the busy Little Quarter Square. One side is a coffee shop, the other is a full service restaurant serving tapas, salads and breakfasts. It's centrally located but always very crowded. *M* to Malostranská **Map p. 84, 3B**

Petřínské terasy Seminářská zahrada 13, 257 320 802. Like the Nebozízek (see below), it is situated half way up Petřín Hill and has stunning views. Stop here if you're nearby, but it's not worth the trek for the food alone. *M* to Malostranská **Map p. 84, 3B**

€€ **Gitanes** Tržiště 7, 257 530 163. Run by a Serb, Gitanes offers homemade soups and tasty Balkan specialities. Best of all, though, is the extraordinary décor, which resembles the interior of a Balkan cottage. *M* to Malostranská **Map p. 84, 3B**

Nebozízek Petřínské sady 411, 257 315 329. The Nebozízek has good-to-variable Czech food combined with breathtaking views of Prague. Get off at the halfway stop on the funicular line, or walk if you feel up to it. *M* to Národní třída or Anděl **Map p. 84, 3C**

Pálffy Palác Valdštejnská 14, 257 530 522. In terms of sheer atmosphere, few Prague restaurants can compete with the Pálffy Palác, an entirely candle-lit Baroque hall with creaking parquet floors and strains of violin music coming from the adjoining conservatoire. Equally romantic is the tiny outdoor terrace, with views over rooftops and gardens. Given the setting, prices could be a lot higher—the €8 and €15 set menus are an absolute bargain. The menu is international cuisine. *M* to Malostranská **Map p. 84, 4A**

U Bílé kuželky Míšeňská 12, 257 535 800. This good-value, no-frills Czech restaurant is attached to a small hotel of the same name. It

Kampa Island

occupies an historic building close to the Charles Bridge. *M* to Malostranská **Map p. 84, 4B**

U Mecenáše Malostránské náměstí 10, 257 531 631. U Mecenáše is one of several long-established places for eating and drinking on the Little Quarter Square, and is good for steaks, Moravian ragout and other hearty Czech fare. The surroundings, though, are somewhat gloomy and cramped. *M* to Malostranská **Map p. 84, 3B**

U Modré kachničky Nebovidská 6, 257 320 308, 257 316 745. The 'Blue Duck' is an atmospheric place to try Czech food, especially roast duck. There are two locations in the city, but this one has a bit more charm. Book a table in the special dining room on the top floor. *M* to Malostranská **Map p. 84, 3B**

U Tří zlatých hvězd Malostránské náměstí 8, 257 531 636. A cheaper alternative to U Mecenáše is U Tří Zlatých Hvězd—and it's certainly better in terms of service. Try the succulent green-pepper steak and other Czech specialities on offer. *M* to Malostranská **Map p. 84, 3B**

€€€ **C'est La Vie** Říční 1, 257 321 511. Riverside dining combined with an innovative kitchen make this a good choice for serious foodies visiting Prague. Look for unusual flavour combinations, like tuna tartare and papadams. The location can't be topped—at the quiet end of Kampa Island away from Little Quarter Square. *M* to Malostranská **Map p. 84, 4C**

Circle Line Malostranské náměstí 12, 257 530 021-3. This is a serious rival to elegant Kampa Park (see below) and has the advantage—usually—of being less crowded. The Circle Line does excellent fish and seafood and a good selection of vegetarian dishes, but service can be slightly fussy. *M* to Malostranská **Map p. 84, 3B**

Hergetova cihelna Cihelná 2b, 257 535 534. The team behind Kampa Park (see below) created this restaurant with an eye towards drawing in crowds that want a more casual and less expensive night out. The view of the Vltava and Charles Bridge is, however, still first class. The excellent wood-fired pizzas, a classy cheeseburger and creative salads have won over Prague regulars. Booking essential. *M* to Malostranská **Map p. 84, 4B**

Kampa Park Na Kampě 8B, 257 532 685. This is Prague's best seafood restaurant and has fantastic views of the Charles Bridge from its riverside terrace. Despite being frequented by visiting film stars, the Kampa is not as expensive as it could be, and prices are more than justified by the delicious, beautifully presented fish specialities and intimate candlelit atmosphere. Booking essential. *M* to Malostranská **Map p. 84, 4B**

U Malířů Maltézské náměstí 11, 257 320 317. The culinary traditions of the 'Painter's House' go back centuries, and today it houses Prague's most exclusive French restaurant. Fresh produce is flown in daily from France and the wine list is entirely French. The food, at prices that few Czechs could afford, is served in beautiful vaulted cellars adorned with 17th-C frescoes. The exquisite Châteaubriand will set you back around €50. *M* to Malostranská **Map p. 84, 3B**

U Maltézských rytířů Prokopská 10, 257 533 666. This is one of the most renowned of the ubiquitous romantically lit 'cellar-style' restaurants. The cuisine is predominantly Czech, with lots of game, fish and poultry dishes, and there is a selection of excellent home-made desserts. Booking advisable. *M* to Malostranská **Map p. 84, 3B**

CAFÉS & TEAHOUSES

Bohemia Bagel Újezd 16. Despite its location on a busy street, this is a good place to refuel before ascending Petřín Hill. There are tables and public telephones outside, internet terminals and a bulletin board within, and, of course, a wide selection of bagels (and spreads) served by friendly English-speaking staff. *M* to Národní třída or Malostranská **Map p. 84, 3B**

Chiméra Lázeňská 6. This ground-floor café, with its neutral, comfortable atmosphere, also has a modest art gallery. It's in the southern half of Malá Strana. *M* to Malostranská **Map p. 84, 3B**

Cukrkávalimonáda Lázeňská 7. A little smoke-free gem, Cukrkávalimonáda offers sandwiches, crêpes and lunchtime specials, as well as good coffee and English-language newspapers. *M* to Malostranská **Map p. 84, 3B**

U Zeleného čaje Nerudova 17. This is an ideal stop-off on your way up to the castle. There are only a few places to sit, but once you get one you can enjoy a wide range of herbal, fruit and black teas. *M* to Malostranská **Map p. 84, 3B**

What you might find at Mýrnyx Týrnyx Retro Vintage

shop

ANTIQUES

Antique Ahasver Prokopská 3, 257 531 404. Ahasver is a must for enthusiasts of vintage clothing, lace, jewellery and knick-knacks. *M* to Malostranská **Map p. 84, 3B**

Vetešnictví Vitězná 12, 257 310 611. This cluttered shop sells a bizarre collection of junk, second-hand goods and genuine antiques. *M* to Anděl **Map p. 84, 4C**

CLOTHES & ACCESSORIES

Karpet Nerudova 18, 225 339 823. No, not carpets—this store sells its own, locally produced hats and caps. The style is more everyday than high-fashion. *M* to Malostranská **Map p. 84, 3B**

Mýrnyx Týrnyx Retro Vintage Móda Saská, 224 923 270. Mýrnyx Týrnyx is a mix of outrageous vintage clothing imported from around the world and the latest creations from cutting-edge Czech designers. Not for the introvert! *M* to Malostranská **Map p. 84, 3B**

GLASS, CERAMICS AND CRAFTS

Galerie Genia Loci Újezd 16, 220 511 163. More a design gallery than a store, Genia Loci sells contemporary glass, porcelain, graphics and furniture made by Italian, German and Czech designers. *M* to Národní třída (across the river) **Map p. 84, 3B**

Galerie Rückl Valdštejnské náměstí 1, 257 171 920. Jan Ryckl founded his glass company in 1846, and the firm is still family-run. The shop specialises in luxurious crystal glass sets, both traditional and modern designs, as well as porcelain and jewellery. *M* to Malostranská **Map p. Map p. 84, 3A**

THE NEW TOWN
(NOVÉ MĚSTO)

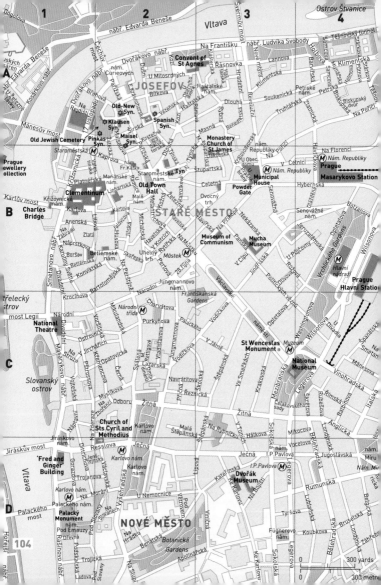

The New Town, which extends south and east of the Staré Město, is the commercial and administrative centre of Prague. It is also the city's main shopping and entertainment district, with an abundance of boutiques, clubs and cinemas, mainly concentrated around the showpiece streets of Národní and Na příkopě. The hub of the Nové Město is the legendary Wenceslas Square (Václavské náměstí), where huge crowds gathered in 1989 to precipitate the 'Velvet Revolution'. Unlike the picturesque Gothic squares of the Old Town, Václavské náměstí—to the surprise of many first-time visitors—has the appearance of some grand Parisian boulevard, with tall 19th-C buildings lining the whole of its 750-metre length. When it was founded by Charles IV in 1348, the New Town was one of the most ambitious examples of town planning in 14th-C Europe. Its medieval street plan is largely preserved, but rapid urban development from the mid-19th C onwards led to the demolition of most of the old houses. In the latter years of the century the city's skyline was enriched by two massive neo-Renaissance buildings that expressed the nationalist aspirations of the Czech people: the National Theatre on Národní avenue and the National Museum on Wenceslas Square. Practically all the leading Czech artists and sculptors of the day worked on the creation of these two magnificent buildings, but even this remarkable achievement was surpassed with the construction in the early years of the 20th C of the Municipal House—a masterpiece of European Art Nouveau and today one of the city's most celebrated buildings.

Municipal House

OPEN	Mon–Sat, 10 am–6 pm
CHARGES	The Concert Hall and Civic Rooms on the first floor can only be visited by guided tour at a cost of 150 Kč per person (no discounts for students or seniors). The English-language tours are at 10.15, 12 pm 2 pm and 4 pm (times subject to change). For information about concert tickets, see p. 151.
TELEPHONE	222 002 100 (Culture and Information Centre)
WEB	www.obecni-dum.cz
MAIN ENTRANCE	náměstí Republiky 5
METRO	náměstí Republiky
DISABLED ACCESS	Yes
SHOP	The Culture and Information Centre, just off the main vestibule, sells tickets for guided tours, books, postcards and souvenirs.
EAT	There is excellent choice of places to eat and drink, including (see p. 119) the Francouzská restaurace and Kavárna Obecní dúm on the ground floor, and the Plzeňská restaurace and American Bar in the basement.

HIGHLIGHTS
Ironwork canopy on the main façade
Francouzská restaurace
Kavárna Obecní dům
Concert Hall
Rieger Hall
Hall of the Lord Mayor

Dominating náměstí Republiky, the Municipal House (Obecní dům) is still the most remarkable Art Nouveau building in the Czech Republic, despite recent restoration that has made its beauty seem somewhat tawdry. It stands on a site originally occupied by the Royal Court of Bohemia, a late 14th-C building that was pulled down in 1902–03. The Municipal House was the brainchild of the Czech Patriotic Society, which envisaged a building that would serve as a social and cultural centre for the Czech community in Prague, complete with café, restaurant,

Municipal House

concert hall, and rooms for civic functions and assemblies. The architects chosen for the task, after a public competition, were Antonín Balšánek and Osvald Polívka. Work on the building was undertaken between 1906 and 1912, and involved the collaboration of many of the leading Czech painters and sculptors of the day, including Ladislav Šaloun, Max Švabinský and, of course, Alfons Mucha. The building saw the proclamation, on October 28, 1918, of the independence of Czechoslovakia as well as the issuing of the new Constitution.

The main façade, overlooking náměstí Republiky, shows a decorative brilliance that crude restoration has fortunately not obscured. It is impressive above all for its central ironwork canopy, coloured with stained glass and topped by bronze figures of lamp-bearers. A door to the right of the vestibule leads into a French restaurant (Francouzská restaurace; see p. 119) with gilded chandeliers, wainscoting and allegorical wall-paintings; to the left of the vestibule is a similarly elegant café (Kavárna Obecní dům; see p. 119) with Art Nouveau furnishings. An ideal place to stop before touring the rest of the building.

The first floor of the Municipal House (access by guided tour only) features the large, ochre-coloured *Smetana Concert Hall*, domed in stained glass. Between the stage and two prominent boxes at the front of the hall are two dynamic sculptural groups by Ladislav Šaloun portraying scenes from Dvořák's *Slavonic Dances* (left) and Smetana's opera *Vyšehrad* (right). Among the other first-floor rooms are the small and exquisitely tasteful neo-Classical pastiche called the *'Sweetshop'*, the rather brasher *Oriental Room* with murals by **Jan Preisler**, and the *Němcová Salon*, decorated all over with stuccowork inspired by folkloric themes.

Pride of place among the Civic Rooms must go to the *Hall of the Lord Mayor*, the windows of which occupy the central position on the building's façade. All the furniture and furnishings and every detail of the decoration of this circular room are by Alfons Mucha, including allegorical murals on the walls and shallow ceiling, the pale-blue stained-glass windows, the Lord Mayor's chair, and the elaborately embroidered curtains.

Mucha Museum

OPEN	10 am–6 pm, daily
CHARGES	120/60 Kč
TELEPHONE	**Museum** 221 451 333
	Shop 224 216 415
WEB	www.mucha.cz
MAIN ENTRANCE	**Kaunitz Palace** Panská 7
METRO	Můstek
DISABLED ACCESS	Yes
SHOP	Good on-site shop selling poster reproductions of Mucha's works and other Mucha-inspired merchandise, including postcards, calendars, books and fashion accessories
EAT	There are plenty of cafés and restaurants in the vicinity of Wenceslas Square.

Alfons Mucha *Princess Hyacinth* (1911)

HIGHLIGHTS
Art Nouveau posters of Sarah Bernhardt
Mucha's decorative designs for stamps and banknotes

Born in 1860 in the Moravian town of Ivančice, Alfons Mucha
showed a prodigiously early talent for draughtsmanship, but none
the less was not accepted into the Prague Academy of Fine Arts.
Apprenticed later as a theatrical scene painter in Vienna, he
stayed there until the burning down of the Ring Theatre in 1880.
Soon after, he attracted the attention of a patron, the Moravian
landowner Count Khuen von Belasi, who arranged for Mucha to
continue his artistic training in Munich and then in Paris.

From his studio on the Rue Val de Grace, Mucha embarked on a
varied artistic career that included oil painting, jewellery and
furniture design. However, his popular reputation was established
above all with his sinuously decorative poster designs, the fame of
which was due initially to a chance commission from the actress
Sarah Bernhardt. Bernhardt was so impressed with the result
that she contracted him to produce posters for all her theatrical
engagements.

After a four-year stay in America, Mucha returned to Bohemia
in 1910, devoting much of his energy to a huge cycle of patriotic
canvases known as the *Slav Epic*. He settled permanently in
Czechoslovakia in 1922, an immensely wealthy and celebrated
artist. He took up residence in Prague's Little Quarter and
continued designing book illustrations, stamps and banknotes. He
died in 1939, at a time when his Art Nouveau whimsicality and
overblown historicism seemed ridiculously old-fashioned. Though
Mucha's popular appeal has been almost continuous since his
death (his richly decorative posters had a special resonance
during the 1960s), his critical reputation declined considerably,
and only began to revive with a large retrospective of his work
held in the Grand Palais in Paris in 1980.

The museum, which opened in 1998, attempts to give an
overview of Mucha's life, with particular emphasis on the period
he spent in Paris (1887-1904), where he produced his most
celebrated work. Indeed, the undoubted highlight of the exhibition

is the large collection of beautiful (and much-reproduced) Art Nouveau posters that Mucha created for the actress Sarah Bernhardt, and which reveal the full sweep of his decorative brilliance; reproductions of these posters are available at the museum shop. Mucha's conception of Art Nouveau is explained through pages from his Parisian sketchbooks and excerpts from *Documents Décoratifs*, a theoretical treatise for artists and craftsmen that he published in 1902.

A separate room is devoted to Mucha's work after his return to Czechoslovakia in 1910, with a selection of oil paintings, pastels and figurative drawings. Far more impressive than these, however, are his exquisite decorative designs for stamps and banknotes issued by the new state of Czechoslovakia after 1918. In the penultimate room, an impoverished attempt is made to

Alfons Mucha *Plate 38 from 'Documents Décoratifs'* (1902)

recreate the atmosphere of Mucha's studio in Paris, using the artist's original chair and easel and some family photographs, including an amusing set of friend and colleague Paul Gauguin. However, this 'studio' gives barely any hint of the world of decorative exuberance in which Mucha actually lived, as anyone who has visited the still-intact Mucha family home at No. 6 Hradčanské náměstí will testify. The exhibition ends with a half-hour video show in English documenting Mucha's life and work, including the genesis of perhaps his greatest work— the monumental *Slav Epic*, now displayed in the Moravian town of Moravský Krumlov.

National Theatre

OPEN	Foyer opens 45 mins before performances; guided tours provided by the Prague Information Service on Sat and Sun during the hours of 8.30 am–11 am
CHARGES	For how to buy tickets, see p. 152.
TELEPHONE	Guided tours (PIS) 221 714 151-2
WEB	www.narodni-divadlo.cz
MAIN ENTRANCE	Národní 2
METRO	Národní třída
DISABLED ACCESS	Yes
EAT	Café Slavia (see p. 121) is across the street.

HIGHLIGHTS
Mythological statues on the main façade
Entrance foyer
Auditorium with its famous back-cloth

One of the great landmarks of Prague, the National Theatre (Národní divadlo) is an eloquent architectural expression of Czech nationalist aspirations in the late 19th C. The painters and sculptors involved in the decoration of the building include almost all the leading Czech artists of the period—they are referred to as 'The National Theatre Generation'. Among the artists were the sculptors Josef Myslbek, Bohuslav Schnirch and Anton Wagner, and the painters Mikoláš Aleš, Václav Brožík, Vojtěch Hynais and František Ženíšek. The creation of the building was financed almost entirely from public donations under the slogan 'The Nation for Itself'.

Despite a fire in 1881 which destroyed the auditorium and much of the building's decorations, the theatre was finally opened on November 18, 1883, with a production of Bedřich Smetana's opera *Libuše*. Exactly 100 years later, after six years of extensive restoration, the same opera marked the reopening of the theatre, which today can be appreciated at its resplendent best.

The National Theatre

THE BUILDING

The grand exterior of the building echoes the Vienna Opera House and, rather more distantly, Renaissance Italy. It is crowned by a Palladian-style roof highlighted by gilding. Some of the finest statuary of the main façade is concentrated on the attic level; there is a row of statues of Apollo and the Muses by **Bohuslav Schnirch**, who also modelled the flanking bronze chariot groups, and on the side façade overlooking the Masaryk Embankment is a portal decorated with reclining figures of Opera and Drama by **Josef Myslbek**.

Inside, a bronze figure by Myslbek representing Music presides over the profusely embellished main foyer, where there are 14 lunette paintings by **Mikoláš Aleš** of scenes from Smetana's symphonic poem, *My Country (Má vlast)*. Of the many other decorations in the building, special mention must be made of the works of **Vojtěch Hynais**. He decorated the stairs leading up to the presidential box with an allegorical frieze, painted vivid representations of the Four Seasons for the ladies' boudoir of the presidential box (note, in particular, the female figure floating over a snow-covered landscape), and provided the stage with its superlative and celebrated backcloth. The backcloth, despite portraying the unpromising theme of 'The Origin of the National Theatre', is full of references to Raphael and Renaissance painting and yet is saved from the absurder excesses of academic art through the sheer energy of the composition and execution. The auditorium is best appreciated during performances—for non-Czech speakers, this means ballet and opera, which feature regularly in the repertoire.

in the area

WENCESLAS SQUARE

National Museum (Národní muzeum) Václavské náměstí 68. Open May–Sept, 10 am–6 pm; Oct–April, 9 am–5 pm. 224 497 111. This vast Neo-Renaissance structure dominates the eastern end of Wenceslas Square. The highlight of the dauntingly large, red-marbled interior is the Pantheon, a room decorated with ambitious historical and allegorical murals by Václav Brožík, František Ženíšek and Vojtěch Hynais, as well as six statues and 42 busts of distinguished Czechs by Josef Myslbek, Ladislav Šaloun, Karel Dvořák and others. The rather unimaginative collections comprise geology, archaeology, prehistory, coins and medals, zoology, palaeontology and anthropology. *M* to Muzeum **Map p. 104, 3-4C**

St Wenceslas Monument Václavské náměstí. Josef Myslbek's masterpiece: an equestrian statue of Wenceslas surrounded by four other patron saints of Bohemia—Sts Ludmila, Procopius, Adalbert and Agnes. During the monument's long gestation (1887–1922) Myslbek's vision of the saint significantly changed. The initial romantic representation of a spiritual leader of the Slavic people was transformed into a sturdy, tightly modelled portrayal of a man embodying the power and authority of the Czech state. David Černý's hilarious parody of the monument, which shows the hapless saint upside down, can be seen in the Lucerna Shopping Arcade, just off the square. *M* to Muzeum **Map p. 104, 3C**

NORTHERN & EASTERN NEW TOWN

Museum of Communism Na příkopě 10. Open daily, 9 am–9 pm. 224 212 966. This tongue-in-cheek exhibition pays ironic homage to the dark days of Communist Czechoslovakia (1948–89). It is the brainchild of American expat businessman Glen Spicker, who trawled the flea markets and junk shops of Prague to amass over a thousand items of memorabilia, including Socialist Realist posters, chemical warfare protection suits, and busts of Marx and Lenin. The display ends with video show of archive footage from the events of 1968 and 1989. *M* to Můstek **Off map p. 104**

Museum of the City of Prague (Muzeum hlavního města Prahy) Na poříčí 52. Open Tues–Sun, 9 am–6 pm. 224 816 772-3. Situated near the noisy Wilsonova flyover, this slightly run-down museum occupies a neo-Renaissance mansion built in 1896–98. The ground floor displays artefacts and art works from the 6th C onwards relating to the history of Prague. On the second floor are the two highlights of the collection: an enormous and fantastically detailed paper model of Prague made between 1826 and 1834, and the original painted calendar executed by Josef Mánes in 1865 for the Astronomical Clock on the Old Town Hall (see p. 13). *M* to Florenc **Off map p. 104**

SOUTHERN & WESTERN NEW TOWN

'Fred and Ginger' Building (Tančící dům) Rašínovo nábřeží 80. This gloriously topsy-turvy structure, intentionally at variance with its sombre neighbours, was designed in 1993–94 by Frank Gehry, architect of the Guggenheim Museum in Bilbao and other cultural landmarks. The curious name derives from the building's resemblance to a dancing couple. On the top floor is a French-run restaurant (La Perle de Prague—see p. 120), which has beautiful views from its rooftop terrace. *M* to Karlovo náměstí **Map p. 104 1D**

Church of Sts Cyril and Methodius (sv. Cyrila a Metoděje) Resslova. Crypt open Tues–Sun, 9 am–4 pm. The church, built by K.I. Dientzenhofer in 1730–36, is famous for its association with one of the most heroic and tragic episodes in the history of the Czech resistance. It was here, in 1942, that the assassins of Reinhard Heydrich, the Nazi Reichsprotektor of Bohemia and Moravia, committed suicide to avoid capture by the SS. The church crypts contain a fascinating and very moving history of the assassination and the conspirators' final stand. A small shrine has been set up where visitors can leave messages and tributes to the men. Outside, the crypt wall is still scarred with bullet holes; there is

Frank Gehry's 'Fred and Ginger' Building

also a memorial shrouded with flowers. *M* to Karlovo náměstí **Map p. 104, 2D**

Palacký Monument Palackého náměstí. The monument in the middle of the square commemorates the 19th-C Czech politician and historian, František Palacký. It is the masterpiece of Myslbek's pupil Stanislav Sucharda (1866–1916), who completed the monument in 1912. A romantic and deeply poetic work, it shows an ingenious use of different materials: the real world—including the heavy, seated figure of Palacký himself—is depicted in stone, the allegorical world in bronze, and the whole composition culminates in a magnificent, asymmetrically placed bronze group soaring above the central stone plinth. *M* to Karlovo náměstí **Map p. 104, 2D**

Dvořák Museum (Muzeum Antonína Dvořáka) Ke Karlovu 20. Open Tues–Sun, 10 am–5 pm. 224 923 363. This modest museum displays personal items, including photographs, scores and a Bösendorfer piano, belonging to the composer Antonín Dvořák, who lived nearby at Žitná 14. Of greater interest, however, is the building itself, a beautiful summer pavilion built by K.I.

Dientzenhofer in 1715–20, set in a small garden adorned with sculptures from the workshop of Matthias Braun; the main room on the first floor, used for chamber concerts (see p. 152), is covered with a delightful illusionistic ceiling painting (c. 1730) by Johann Ferdinand Schor. *M* to I.P. Pavlova **Map p. 104, 3D**

commercial galleries

Czech Photography Centre Náplavní 1, 224 922 726. Open daily, 11 am–6 pm. Good exhibitions of modern Czech photography in attractive, if rather cramped, surroundings. *M* to Karlovo náměstí **Map p. 104, 1C**

Galerie Pyramida Národní 11, 224 213 117, www.i-gallery.cz. Open daily, 10.30 am–7 pm. One of the largest commercial art galleries in Prague, representing approximately 500 Czech and Slovak artists. The focus is mainly on bronze and glass sculpture, as well as painting and graphic art. *M* to Národní třída **Map p. 104, 1C**

Galerie Tvrdohlaví Vodičkova 36 (Lucerna Palace), 296 236 491, www.tvrdohlavi.cz (in Czech). Open daily, 10 am–10 pm. A gallery devoted to the Tvrdohlaví ('Stubborn Ones') art group, whose members include Jiří David, Michal Gabriel, Čestmír Suška and Petr Nikl. *M* to Můstek **Map p. 104, 3C**

Gambit Mikulandská 6, 224 910 508. Open Mon–Sat, 12 pm–6 pm. A tiny gallery showing new works by leading Czech sculptors and painters. *M* to Národní třída **Map p. 104, 2C**

Jiří Švestka Gallery Biskupský dvůr 6, 222 311 092, www.jiri svestka.com. Open, Tue–Fri, 12 pm–6 pm; Sat, 11 am–6 pm. Prague's best commercial gallery, and the only one that participates in international art fairs. It is also the only commercial venue in the Czech Republic that showcases foreign artists of international note. One room within the gallery space is dedicated to works amassed by the famous Czech collector Vincenc Kramář, whose estate the gallery represents. Kramář was collecting in the early half of the 20th C, and is credited with having recognised the talent of Picasso well before the rest of the art world. The majority of the collection now hangs in the Trade Fair Palace (see p. 131), but what remains with the family (including Picasso prints,

Gutfreund sculptures and Kupka paintings) is shown here in the Kramář room on a rotating basis. There is also a well-stocked English-language art bookshop on the premises. *M* to náměstí Republiky or Florenc **Map p. 104, 4A**

Mánes Exhibition Hall Masarykovo nábřeží 250, 224 930 754, www.nadace-cfu.cz. Open Tue–Sun, 10 am–6 pm. A riverside gallery sponsored by the Czech Fund for Art Foundation. The Functionalist building, which straddles the narrow stretch of water between the Slavonic Island (Slovanský ostrov) and the Masaryk Embankment, was erected by Otakar Novotný in 1923–25. The gallery puts on exhibitions by Czech artists of varying quality and holds occasional multimedia shows. There is also a café and dance club with seating on the terrace. *M* to Karlovo náměstí **Map p. 104, 1C**

Václav Špála Gallery Národní třída 30, 224 946 738, www.nadace-cfu.cz. Open Tue–Sun, 10 am–12 pm and 12.30 pm–6 pm. A spacious and popular venue sponsored by the Czech Fund for Art Foundation. It has monthly exhibitions of contemporary Czech art on the ground and first floors, with installations by lesser-known talents in the basement. *M* to Národní třída **Map p. 104, 2C**

eat

AT THE MUSEUMS

€€ **Kavárna Obecní Dům** náměstí Republiky 5. This showpiece café, with its grand Art Nouveau interior, is located inside the Municipal House (see p. 106). Lunches served; otherwise it's definitely a place worth stopping to take some time for a coffee. *M* to náměstí Republiky **Map p. 104, 3B**

Plzeňská restaurace náměstí Republiky 5 (Obecní dům), 222 002 770. Average Czech cuisine served in the basement of the beautiful Municipal House (see p. 106). The interior is done in the style of a beer hall, enlivened with ceramic decoration and stained glass. *M* to náměstí Republiky **Map p. 104, 3B**

€€€ **Francouzská restaurace** náměstí Republiky 5 (Obecní dům), 222 002 770. Francouzská serves French cuisine in a splendid Art

Nouveau interior, with gilded chandeliers, wainscotting and allegorical wall paintings. Guests can chose from the à la carte, gourmet or 'surprise' menus, the latter consisting of seven courses selected by the chef. Booking advisable. *M* to náměstí Republiky **Map p. 104, 3B**

SURROUNDING AREA

€ **Kmotra V** Jirchářích 12, 224 934 100. This pizzeria is an excellent choice for cheap, well-made pizzas and pasta dishes. They've even been successful enough to open a second branch. *M* to Národní třída **Map p. 104, 2C**

Pizza Coloseum Vodičkova 32, 224 214 914. Avoid the KFC at street level and head straight down to the cellars for a first-rate pizza experience. Not only are the pizzas delicious, the atmosphere is suprisingly comfortable. *M* to Můstek **Map p. 104, 3C**

€€ **Le Bistrot de Marlene** Plavecká 4, 224 921 853. Slightly off the beaten track, this French restaurant serves up classic fare like baked leeks and duck confit, all in a cosy setting. The menu changes seasonally and the wine list is well-chosen. *M* to Karlovo náměstí **Map p. 104, 1D**

Miyabi Navrátilova 10, 296 233 102. This restaurant and tearoom is situated in a quiet backstreet near to the birthplace of Jaroslav Hašek. The Miyabi, run by a Czech woman who lived for many years in Japan, offers a curious and delicious mixture of Czech and Japanese cuisine. *M* to Karlovo náměstí **Map p. 104, 2C**

Radost FX Café Bělehradská 120, 224 254 776. A short walk from the National Museum (see p. 115), the Radost is known primarily as a fashionable dance club. However, the ground-floor café is a haven for vegetarians exasperated with the bland, stodgy veg options served in Czech restaurants. The menu offers a wide selection of vegetarian cuisine arranged by country—from Italian and Greek to French, American and Moroccan. Lunchtimes are particularly busy; later, clubbers refuel on the pasta dishes that are served through the night. *M* to I.P. Pavlova **Map p. 104, 4D**

Zahrada v Opeře (Opera Garden) Legerova 75, 224 239 685. Tucked away behind the State Opera building (Státní opera), this airy restaurant has an attractive minimalist décor and an international menu that also caters to vegetarians. *M* to Muzeum **Map p. 104, 4C**

€€€ **La Perle de Prague** Rašínovo nábřeží 80, 221 984 160. Located on the 7th floor of the extraordinary 'Fred and Ginger' building (see p.

116), this restaurant offers good-to-excellent French food complemented by breathtaking views from its roof terrace. Unfortunately, the service can be rather frosty if you're not prepared to splash out. Booking advisable. *M* to Karlovo náměstí **Map p. 104, 1D**

Ostroff Střelecký ostrov 336, 224 919 235. Refined Italian cuisine is served at this popular establishment with a superb location on Shooter's Island. Preface your meal with sophisticated cocktail drinks at the bar. *M* to Národní třída **Map p. 104, 1C**

CAFÉS & TEAHOUSES

Café Imperial Na poříčí 15. The Imperial boasts an impressive, if now slightly worn, Art Nouveau interior with wood panelling and ornate ceramic decoration. It's best avoided on hot days, though, as there's no air-conditioning to speak of, nor any seating outside, and it's situated on a busy thoroughfare. *M* to náměstí Republiky **Map p. 104, 4A**

Café Arco Dlážděná 6. In its early 20th-C heyday, this famed establishment was a meeting place for Prague's artistic and literary élite, with Brod, Werfel and Kafka among its regulars. Now it's a downmarket café and busy lunchtime eatery, convenient if you're travelling to or from Masarykovo station. *M* to náměstí Republiky **Map p. 104, 4B**

Globe Bookstore and Coffeehouse Pštrossova 6, 224 934 203. This legendary expat institution was founded at a time when Americans saw Prague as the height of cool and flocked here in their multitudes. The Globe's new premises are more sterile and somewhat less welcoming than the old, but this is still a good place to rub shoulders with Prague's (foreign) literary personalities. The bulletin board and high-tech Internet terminals are particularly handy, and you can hang out in the relaxed lunch bar/café. *M* to Národní třída **Map p. 104, 1C**

Café Slavia Národní 1. A famous riverside café, the Slavia has been a meeting place for writers and artists since the early 20th C, and has featured in the works of Rilke, Seifert, Havel and others. Nowadays, the former stalwarts have been replaced by tourists and theatre-goers, but the Slavia still exudes a distinctly unreconstructed feel—the décor, and particularly the service, have failed to move with the times. Don't bother eating here, and be sure to get a table on the embankment side for a picture-postcard view of the castle. *M* to Národní třída **Map p. 104, 1C**

Café Louvre Národní 20. Traditionalists will enjoy this imposing turn-of-the-last-century café located in the same building as the famous Reduta jazz club (see p. 152). There's a pool hall at the back and windows at the front overlooking one of Prague's main shopping streets. *M* to Národní třída **Map p. 104, 2C**

Velryba Opatovická 24. Velryba is a large basement café with a very young clientele who come for the dirt-cheap lunches and sociable atmosphere. *M* to Národní třída **Map p. 104, 2C**

shop

BOOKS

Academia Václavské náměstí 34, 224 223 511. This centrally located bookshop has a small English-language section and an upstairs café. It stocks maps, magazines, guides, language books and fiction. *M* to Můstek **Map p. 104, 3C**

Globe Bookstore and Coffeehouse Pštrossova 6, 224 934 203. At this renowned expat lunch bar/café, you can also sink into a comfortable armchair and peruse the diverse selection of new and second-hand books and foreign-language magazines. *M* to Národní třída **Map p. 104, 1C**

Kanzelsberger Václavské náměstí 4, 224 219 214. A huge chain bookshop, Kanzelberger has a foreign-language section (including Czech literature in translation) on the top floor. CDs, games, videos and maps are also available. Ask the knowledgeable staff if you can't find what you want. *M* to Můstek **Map p. 104, 3B**

CLOTHES & ACCESSORIES

Delmas Vodičkova 36 (Lucerna Shopping Arcade), 224 239 132. A wide range of moderately priced leather goods and accessories, including chic Italian designer handbags as well as wallets, purses, gloves, belts, briefcases and satchels. *M* to Můstek or Muzeum **Map p. 104, 3C**

Galerie Módy Heleny Fejkové Štěpánská 61 (Lucerna Shopping Arcade, first floor), 224 211 514. This difficult-to-find boutique showcases the

Local design from Taiza

latest creations of Helena Fejková and other Prague designers, with a good jewellery selection at the back. There's also an on-site café. *M* to Můstek **Map p. 104, 3C**

Senior Bazar Senovážné náměstí 18, 224 235 068. Not a place to look for new grandparents; it's one of the best places to buy vintage and second-hand clothes. Come early to avoid the hordes of bargain-hunters. *M* to náměstí Republiky **Map p. 104, 4B**

Taiza Na příkopě 31, 225 113 308. Glamour, sex appeal and fresh and creative elegance characterise the fashion-forward designs of Taiza. Started by Cuban emigré Osmany Laffita, Taiza is a player on the local fashion scene that shouldn't be missed. *M* to Můstek **Map p. 104, 3B**

123

FOOD

Jan Paukert Národní 17, 224 232 466. This popular Czech deli, established in 1916, offers delicious open-faced sandwiches (chlebíčky) as well as local wines and spirits and an array of imported cheeses. *M* to Národní třída **Map p. 104, 2C**

GLASS, CERAMICS & CRAFTS

Alfa Galerie Národní 43, 224 222 865. Alfa Galerie sells Czech handicrafts, with an emphasis on porcelain and ceramics, including colourful hand-painted tea sets. *M* to Národní třída or Můstek **Map p. 104, 2B**

Artěl Vinohradská 164, 271 732 161. The brainchild of American designer Karen Feldman, who moved to Prague in 1994. Artel—unlike many other glass retailers—focuses on traditional glassmaking techniques and high standards of workmanship. The beautiful etched and blown products are displayed in an Art Deco revival salon, open by appointment only. *M* to náměstí Míru **Off map p. 104**

Keramika Národní 19, 224 219 210. This shop has a large selection of good value, modern handcrafted pottery, available as individual items or complete sets. *M* to Národní třída or Můstek **Map p. 104, 2C**

JEWELLERY

Art Décoratif U Obecního domu 1, 222 002 350. Situated around the corner from the famous Municipal House (see p. 106), this shop is itself a temple of Art Nouveau, complete with parquet floors, wall hangings and wooden display cases containing well-crafted reproductions of Art Nouveau jewellery, glassware and other gift items. *M* to náměstí Republiky **Map p. 104, 2A**

Preciosa Jindřišská 19, 222 247 406. Preciosa is an established global company selling luxury fashion jewellery with stones cut from glass or cubic zirconium, as well as exquisite crystal chandeliers and cut crystal figurines. *M* to Můstek or Muzeum **Map p. 104, 3B**

Prague Diamond 2000 Na příkopě 31 and Maiselova 21, 224 811 011. The shop sells an elegant selection of diamond, gold and platinum jewellery mostly produced in the on-site workshop. *M* to Můstek (for Na příkopě branch), to Staroměstská (for Maiselova branch) **Map p. 104, 3B** (for Na příkopě branch) and **Map p. 104, 2A** (for Maiselova branch)

Vily Václavské náměstí 13, 224 227 476. Vily specialises in mostly Italian-made gold jewellery. *M* to Můstek **Map p. 104, 3B**

MUSIC

234 Bělehradská 120, 224 252 741. Situated next to the Radost café and dance club (see p. 155), this small shop has an excellent and very reasonably priced selection of alternative music, with further sections devoted to dance, jazz and world music. *M* to IP Pavlova **Map p. 104, 4D**

AghaRTA Krakovská 5, 222 211 275. AghaRTA offers an excellent selection of jazz CDs from around the world. It's located inside a club of the same name. *M* to Muzeum **Map p. 104, 3C**

Bontonland Jungmannova 20, 246 08 61 50. This is one of the best shops for cheap classical music CDs, and is the classical outpost of the larger Bontonland (see below). *M* to Národní třída or Můstek **Map p. 104, 2C**

Bontonland Megastore Václavské náměstí 1 (Koruna Palace), 224 226 236. This was the first Western-style megastore in the Czech Republic, and it's still the biggest. The megastore stocks dance, rock and pop CDs as well as a fairly good selection of jazz and classical. There's also an internet café, computer game zones, and even an in-store DJ. *M* to Můstek **Map p. 104, 3B**

Jazz Meets World Dittrichova 11, 224 922 830. Stop at this store for rare recordings of European jazz. Good for the collector or true aficionado. *M* to Karlovo náměstí **Map p. 104, 1D**

Tamizdat RPM Jindřišská 5, 222 240 934. This shop specialises in independent and alternative music from Central and Eastern Europe. It's located in the fourth-floor café of the Unijazz organisation, which sponsors festivals of new and interesting music. *M* to Můstek **Map p. 104, 3B**

SHOES

Bat'a Václavské náměstí 6, 224 218 133. This famous global brand in shoes was founded by Czech industrialist Tomáš Bát'a (1876–1932) in the late 19th C. Nationalised after World War II, Bát'a stores have now returned to the Czech Republic and are one of the best places to buy good quality footwear. The showpiece store on Wenceslas Square is inside a newly refurbished 1920s Functionalist building designed by Ludvík Kysela. *M* to Můstek **Map p. 104, 3B**

Beltissimo Na příkopě 22 (Slovanský dům), 221 451 245. Beltissimo sells shoes and other leather speciality items, and carries a wide selection of Italian, French and German brands. *M* to Můstek or náměstí Republiky **Map p. 104, 3B**

Humanic Národní třída 34, 224 920 560. This very popular Austrian-owned chain has an extensive selection of shoes aimed at the younger end of the market. You get what you pay for with low prices, low quality. *M* to Můstek or Národní třída **Map p. 104, 2C**

Vagabond Na příkopě 19 (Myslbek Shopping Arcade), 224 232 234. This Scandinavian company has a reputation for hard-wearing yet stylish and inexpensive footwear. It has several well-stocked shops around Prague, offering everything from trainers and sandals to boots and heels. *M* to Můstek **Map p. 104, 3B**

SPORT

Calcio CZ Myslíkova 30, 224 917 347. If you're looking for ice hockey or football merchandise—for example, the official shirts of the Czech national team—then this is the place for you. *M* to Karlovo náměstí **Map p. 104, 2C**

Giga Sport Na příkopě 19-21 (Myslbek Shopping Arcade), 224 233 552. Giga is the biggest sports shop in Prague, with a vast selection of winter and summer sports equipment and clothing. *M* to Můstek or náměstí Republiky **Map p. 104, 3B**

WINE & BEER

Cellarius Štěpánská 61 (Lucerna Shopping Arcade), 224 210 979. This shop stocks fine Moravian wines, including some very rare vintages, which you can sample at the relaxed on-site wine bar. Though the shop boasts 1,300 imported wines, these are of varying quality and generally overpriced. *M* to Můstek or Muzeum **Map p. 104, 3C**

Dionýsos Vinařického 6, T 224 922 237. An upmarket wine merchant with a fantastic selection of top-quality local wines, Dionýsos has helpful English-speaking staff and a delivery service. *M* to Karlovo náměstí **Off map p. 104**

La Casa de Cigarros y del Vino Na příkopě 12 (Černá růže Shopping Arcade), 221 014 716. You can find a decent selection of domestic and international wines here, but most visitors come for the Cuban cigars. *M* to Můstek **Map p. 104, 3B**

THE TRADE FAIR
PALACE &
TROJA CHÂTEAU

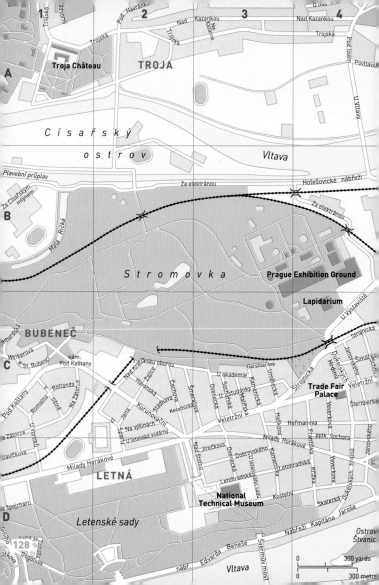

1   **2**   **3**   **4**

Trojská

Na Havránce

Nad Kazankou

Na Kazance

Nad Kazankou

Trojská

Trojská

Trojská

Pod líseň

Povltavská

A   Troja Château   **TROJA**

U Vltavy

C í s a ř s k ý

o s t r o v   Vltava

Plavební průplav

Za Císařským mlýnem

Za elektrárnou

Holešovické nábřeží

B

Za elektrárnou

Malá Rická

S t r o m o v k a   **Prague Exhibition Ground**

Lapidarium

U Výstaviště

Strojnická

BUBENEČ

Gotthardská

Wolkerova

nám.
Pod Kaštany

Pod Král'ovskou oborou

Gerstnerova

Jankovského

Šimáčko

U Smíchc

C   St. Bubenče

Nad Královskou oborou

U akademie

Umělecká

Dukelských
Hrdinů

Veletržní

Na Zátorce

Romaina

Iišhé

Rottanda

Havlanská

Za Elánku

Čechova

Šmeralova

Dientzenhoferova

Kamenická

Strojnická

**Trade Fair
Palace**

Sternberk

Pod Kaštany

Romaina

U Jana

Sládkova

Keramická

U studánky

Malířská

Janovského

Veverkova

Za Zátorce

U vorníků

Korunovační

Na výšinách

Ovenecká

Veletržní

Haškova

Heřmanova

Františka

Milady Horákové

pplk. Sochora

Stavitelská

U letenské vodárny

Nad Štolou

Jirečkova

Ovenecká

Dobrovského

Kamenická

Letohradská

Krká

Dukelských

Janovského

LETNÁ

Milady Horákové

Letohradská

Letohradská

**National
Technical Museum**

Kostelní

Skalecká

Dukelských

Jaroše

D   *Letenské sady*

Ostrov
Štvanice

U špejcharu

Bogota

nábř. Edvarda Beneše

Šermu most

Nábřeží Kapitána

Vltava

0   300 yards

0   300 metre

Nestled in a bend of the Vltava, the district of Holešovice has a rather unprepossessing feel, especially when compared to the architectural wonders of the city centre. Until the 19th C, it was little more than an outlying village, but with industrialisation it gradually acquired factories, workers' tenements, and a new bridge—the Hlákův most—linking it with the New Town to the south. In 1869, Holešovice was annexed to the neighbouring village of Bubeneč, before being fully incorporated into Prague in 1884. Its greatest moment came in 1891, when it was chosen as the venue for the Jubilee Industrial Exhibition, where the latest technological innovations were shown off in a specially constructed exhibition ground (Výstaviště). Nowadays, Holešovice is resolutely residential, but it manages to draw tourists on account of the Trade Fair Palace (Veletržní palác), the first Functionalist building of its scale in Europe, now stunningly adapted to house the modern art collections of the National Gallery.

Holešovice's other selling point is the large and wooded Stromovka Park, which borders the exhibition ground to the west. From the Stromovka you can make an enjoyable 30-minute walk via the footbridges on Emperor's Island (Císařský ostrov) to the suburban district of Troja. Here, a large Baroque country house—the Troja Château (Trojský zámek)—provides an attractive setting for the Prague City Gallery's collection of 19th-C Czech paintings. The rooms of the Château look out over a French formal garden, with terraces sloping down to the river—a excellent spot for an afternoon stroll.

National Gallery at the Trade Fair Palace

OPEN	Tues–Sun, 10 am–6 pm
CHARGES	The permanent exhibitions cover four floors, but partial tickets can be bought. All four floors: 250/120 Kč. Choice of any three floors: 200/100 Kč. Choice of any two floors: 150/50 Kč. Any one floor: 100/50 Kč. Family ticket: 300 Kč. Admission is free on public holidays; the ground, mezzanine and fifth floors host temporary exhibitions for which separate tickets are required.
TELEPHONE	224 301 024; general information about exhibitions: 222 321 459
WEB	www.ngprague.cz
MAIN ENTRANCE	Dukelských hrdinů 47
METRO	Vltavská
DISABLED ACCESS	Yes
GUIDED VISITS	Tours in English, French or German are organised by the National Gallery's education departments; 1200 Kč for groups up to 15 persons; 1500 Kč for groups over 15 persons; standard admission is also payable. 224 301 003
SHOP	Bookshop with a wide range of art, design and photography books as well as exhibition catalogues and guides
EAT	There is a modest restaurant at the rear section of the palace and an Internet café to the left of the foyer

HIGHLIGHTS

Gustav Klimt's *The Virgin*

Oscar Kokoschka's views of Prague

Zdeněk Pešánek's *Recumbent Torso*

František Kupka's *Piano Keys–Lake*

Cézanne's *House in Aix; portrait of Joachim Gasquet*

Gauguin's *Good-day Mr Gauguin*

Mikoláš Aleš' *The Meeting of George of Poděbrady with Matthias Corvinus*

Jakub Schikaneder's *All Souls Say; Sorrowful Homecoming; Evening Interior*

The Functionalist lines of the Trade Fair Palace

THE BUILDING

The enormous success of the Jubilee Industrial Exhibition of 1891 highlighted the need among Czech politicians and businessmen for an annual trade fair at the heart of what had by now become the Habsburg Empire's most industrial region. However, it was not until the birth of Czechoslovakia that a Prague Trade Fair Committee was finally established. After two competitions, the architects Oldřich Tyl and Josef Fuchs were assigned the task of creating the Trade Fair Palace.

Between 1926 and 1928, they created a building designed to hold 10,000 visitors and 4,000 exhibitors. In addition to administrative offices, corridors with 'shop bays' and a Great Hall, the palace featured an elegant restaurant and a 600-seat cinema. Among the first visitors was Le Corbusier, who claimed that the building showed him how Functionalism could be applied on a pioneeringly vast scale. The palace maintained its original purpose until 1951, when the Prague Trade Fair was closed down. A fire in 1974 caused major damage, and reconstruction of the building was not completed until 20 years later.

With the opening of the National Gallery's Collection of Modern Art at the Trade Fair Palace, Prague has gained not only an attraction rivalling any of its older monuments, but also one of Europe's most exciting new galleries. The vitality, originality and exhilarating freshness of the building is exemplified above all in the pristinely white atrium. This luminous sky-lit hall, situated at the northern end of the palace, is surrounded by balconied galleries that, on one side, form an inwardly sloping wall of railings reminiscent of the hull of some futuristic ocean liner of Titanic proportions. The galleries themselves are lined with lively modern sculptures and applied art that complement the paintings displayed in the main section of the building.

THE COLLECTION
FIRST FLOOR *20th-C Foreign art*

The foreign-school holdings on the first floor are particularly notable for their fine German and Austrian works dating mainly

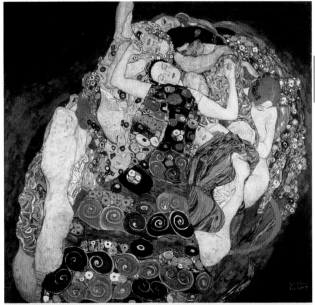

Gustav Klimt *The Virgins* (1913)

from the first three decades of the 20th C. Among the former are **Max Ernst**'s *Life in a House* (1919), *Still-Life with Flowers* and *Envelope* (1922) by **Corinth**, Expressionist canvases by **Schmidt-Rottluff** and **Pechstein**, and a disturbing work by the undeservedly little-known **Max Oppenheimer** entitled *The Operation*, which shows an hysterical group of hands and scalpels.

The Austrian holdings are dominated by superb paintings by **Schiele**, **Klimt** and **Kokoschka**. Schiele is represented by a small townscape of 1911 (a view of Český Krumlov, the birthplace of Schiele's mother) and a haunting tall canvas of a monk and a woman, entitled *Pregnant Woman and Death* (1911). **Klimt**'s *The Virgins* (1913) is a large decorative composition in vivid blues and

NATIONAL GALLERY AT THE TRADE FAIR PALACE

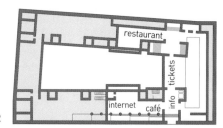

GROUND FLOOR

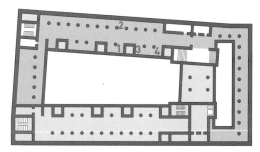

FIRST FLOOR 20th-C Foreign Art

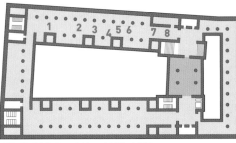

SECOND FLOOR Czech Art 1930–2000

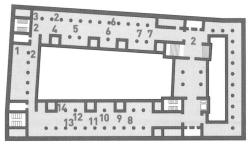

THIRD FLOOR Czech Art 1900–1930

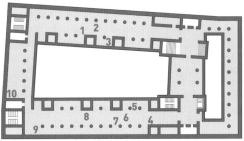

FOURTH FLOOR 19th-C Art

purples, showing an entwined group of female nudes (see above).
Also by Klimt is a landscape (*Castle with a Moat*, 1909) and an
armchair he designed for the Primavesi Villa (1905).

Kokoschka lived in Prague in 1934–35, and there are several
works by him from this period. Pride of place must go to three
large and expressively painted views of Prague from the river,
constituting possibly the finest landscapes ever made of this city.
Another fine work is the amusing *Red Eggs* (1939), which looks like
something out of *Alice's Adventures in Wonderland*.

The foreign artist whose work was of most relevance to the
development of early-20th-C Czech art was **Edvard Munch**, who is
represented here by only two works, the best being a highly
atmospheric painting of a group of women dancing on a shore by
moonlight (1900).

SECOND FLOOR *Art from 1930 to the present day*

Much of the space on the second floor is taken up with the
delicate dream-like Surrealism of painters who came to the fore
in the 1920s, such as the versatile **Jindřich Štyrský** and the
morphological painters **Toyen** and **Josef Šíma**. More arresting and
memorable examples of the influence of Surrealism are 1930s
assemblages by **Zdeněk Rykr** and **Ladislav Zívr**. Rykr used glass
boxes in which he assembled a mixture of treated paper and
unorthodox (and often ephemeral) materials such as thread,
cotton wool, wood and silver foil (as in his *Orient* series of 1935).
Zívr also improvised from random materials but in a more three-
dimensional and morbid way, as in his *Heart Incognito* (1936), in
which a heart-like object is trapped in netting above a black vase.
But the prize for originality must be awarded to the kinetic light
sculptures of **Zdeněk Pešánek**, whose principal work on this floor
is *Recumbent Torso*. This luminous, welded blend of plastic, glass,
neon and lightbulbs formed part of a fountain exhibited at the
World Exhibition of Art and Technology in Paris in 1937, and is like
an avant-garde response to the Venus de Milo.

Surrealism continued to dominate the work of the avant-garde
(and often censored) Czech artists of the 1940s and later, such as
Mikuláš Medek. But the works on the second floor that have
perhaps the greatest appeal today are the haunting urban

landscapes of **Jan Smetana**, such as *Last Stop* (1944); **František Gross**'s ironically titled *Garden of Eden* (1943); and, above all, the works of **Kamil Lhoták**, which are a perfect blend of realism, poetry, colouristic subtlety and arresting imagery, notably *Officer's Mess in Paris* (1947) and *Baseball Player* (1947).

The gallery's modern-art section has been expanded in recent years to take the story right up to the present day, but the sheer quantity of exhibits can overwhelm the visitor. There is an amusing collection of Socialist Realist art, including edifying images of 'heroic' proletarians and models of limousines used by party apparatchiks. Also interesting are examples of the roughly contemporaneous Art Informel, Europe's answer to Abstract Expressionism. Brief tribute is paid to Czech performance art of the 1960s, which is followed by some of the Surrealistic photomontages for which **Jiří Kolář** is famous. The final section displays works, of varying quality, by 'underground' artists active in Czechoslovakia during the 1980s, some of whom went on to greater things after the 'Velvet Revolution'.

THIRD FLOOR *Czech art 1900–1930*

The gallery's large and intriguing collection of early-20th-C Czech painting covers all the leading artists of the period. Perhaps the greatest influence on this generation was the Norwegian **Edvard Munch**. A retrospective of Munch's work held in 1905 in Prague's Mánes Gallery led to the formation of the *Osma* ('The Eight') art movement, whose members included **Václav Špála**, **Emil Filla** and **Bohumil Kubišta**. Works such as Špála's fiery *Self-Portrait with Palette* (1908), Filla's spiritually tormented *Reader of Dostoyevsky* (1907) and Kubišta's sinisterly green *Cardplayers* (1909) are pure homages to the Norwegian artist.

These three painters, together with **Otakar Kubín**, **Antonín Procházka** and **Josef Čapek**, later embraced no less whole-heartedly the Cubist works of Picasso and Braque. Many of their Cubist paintings are virtually indistinguishable from the art of their French peers except for the occasional Czech lettering and identifiable landscapes, as in, for instance, Kubišta's *Quarry in Braník* (1910–11) and Filla's *Still Life with Art Monthly* (1914).

A far more idiosyncratic painter than any of these was the deeply spiritual artist **Jan Zrzavý**, some of whose early works, such as *The Anti-Christ* (1909), display a powerfully expressive use of colour and brushstroke. At the same time, he began developing a completely different style, characterised by strange doll-like figures and an almost naively simple handling of paint and composition: one of the earliest such paintings was his *Valley of Sorrow* (1908), which he later described as being imbued with all his sense of 'sadness and hopelessness'.

The most original and truly outstanding Czech painter of these years was **František Kupka**. His works on show here reveal his development from a Fauve-like manner—in, for instance, *Cabaret Actress* (1909–10)—to the pioneering abstract compositions of 1911 onwards, such as the fluently lyrical blue and red *Fugue in Two Colours* (1912). A sensational transitional work—and one that first reveals the influence of music on his art—is *Piano Keys-Lake* (1909), in which reflections on water are effortlessly transformed into the keys of a piano.

With a move into pure abstraction two years later, Kupka experimented with what he called 'cosmic architecture', which is demonstrated here in a series of ambitious canvases begun in 1911–13 and reworked at the beginning of the 1920s. Some resemble coloured and fractured organ pipes, such as his *Perpendicular and Transverse Surfaces* (1913–23) or *Colour Planes, Winter Recollection* (1913–23). A literal climax to his art is reached in the magnificent *Story about Pistils and Stamens, 1* (1920), which has been described as a 'depiction of a cosmic sexual act'. From the 1930s onwards, Kupka's art became more academic and rigorously geometric; in *Abstract Painting* (1930), for instance, a white canvas is marked with one vertical and two horizontal black lines; not even Mondrian could match such minimalism.

The early 20th-C Czech paintings are interspersed with applied art and a vast collection of sculptures by **Otto Gutfreund**, who dominated Czech 20th-C sculpture in the same way that Myslbek had presided over the preceding century. Gutfreund began his career in a Cubist vein (for instance, the bronze *Head of Viki*,

1912–13, and *Anxiety*, 1911–12) but later went on to develop a very realistic yet highly personal style devoted to the portrayal of the everyday world. These latter works were characterised by simple, stately forms and a complete lack of sentimentality, as in the bronze *Family* (1925). Gutfreund often made use of colour, as, for instance, in the terracotta *Self-Portrait* (1919) and the groups *Industry* and *Commerce* (both 1923), in wood and plaster respectively. They represent a truly Czech style of sculpture and their so-called Objective Realism was to be emulated by numerous other artists.

French art of the 19th and 20th centuries

Many of the works in the collection of French art were amassed by Vincenc Kramář, the enlightened director of the National Gallery during the 1920s. He was forced to 'donate' his collection to the gallery in 1960, a few months before his death at the age of 83. Among the artists represented are **Delacroix** (*Jaguar Attacking a Horseman*, 1855), **Pissarro** (an excellent view of Pontoise, before 1870), **Renoir** (*The Lovers*, 1875), **Monet** (*Ladies Among Flowers*, 1875), **Degas** (*Portrait of Lorenzo Pagans*, 1882), **Van Gogh** (*Green Wheat*, 1889–90), **Cézanne** (*House in Aix*, 1885–87, and a superlative portrait of the Pontoise doctor, patron and friend to the Impressionists, Joachim Gasquet, 1896–97), **Gauguin** (the famous Pont-Aven parody of Courbet, *Good-Day Mr Gauguin*, 1889), **Rodin** (three bronze busts and a bronze maquette of his Balzac monument), **Toulouse-Lautrec** (*Moulin-Rouge*, 1892), and **Le Douanier Rousseau** (this artist's only known self-portrait, 1890).

Kramář's greatest contribution to the arts in Czechoslovakia was his early championing of Cubism. He bought works in Paris in the first and second decades of the 20th C that would profoundly influence a whole generation of avant-garde Czech artists and architects. Thanks to Kramář, the National Gallery has a **Picasso** and **Braque** collection unrivalled in Central Europe. The Picassos (which, due to the chronological arrangement of the collections, are spread out over the first three floors) include two paintings belonging to his so-called Negro Period (a *Self-Portrait* of 1907 and a *Female Head* of the same year), a large group of 'analytical Cubist' works of 1910 and 1911, and some 'synthetic Cubist' works of 1912 and 1913. There are also later purchases, such as his monumental *Standing Nude* of 1921, as well as works on loan from other museums, such as *The Rape of the Sabine Women* (1962; Museum of Fine Arts in Boston). Braque's career is traced from the analytical Cubist period of 1910–11—when his works were virtually identical to Picasso's of these years—to the development of his very lyrical and painterly still-lifes of the 1920s. Among the other Cubist paintings are early works by **Derain**, most notably a view of Cadaqués of 1910; Derain's later manner is represented by a sturdy and very Classical *Seated Woman* of 1920.

FOURTH FLOOR *19th-century art*
This floor is devoted almost exclusively to 19th-C Czech paintings that provide valuable insight into the subject matter that has always preoccupied Czech nationalists.

It begins with the more important Czech artists of the early 19th C, including **Ludvík Kohl**, painter of romantic Gothic interiors, and **Antonín Machek**, who delicately portrayed the leading figures associated with the nationalist revival. Two other major names are **Josef Navrátil**—the author of a stunningly simple and realistic series of still-lifes—and **Antonín Mánes**, who is represented here by a number of romantic landscapes imbued with nationalist sentiment.

Two of Mánes's sons were painters, the most famous being the elder, **Josef Mánes**, whose work dominates Czech 19th-C art. The paintings on show here reveal his extraordinary range, from such academic canvases as *Petrarch and Laura* (1845–46) to a series of remarkably fresh landscapes painted in the 1850s and 1860s (for instance *View of Gmunden* and *Mountain Hut*).

Of Mánes's younger contemporaries, the only one to achieve an international reputation was **Jaroslav Čermák**, who specialised in ambitious scenes of Czech history, such as *The Hussites Defending the Pass* (1857). Čermák, a Byronic figure with the painterly pretensions of a Delacroix, became an active witness to history by going off to record the war between Turkey and Montenegro, the subject of several scenes here, including *Captives* (1870).

Towards the end of the 19th C many of the leading Czech artists were engaged in the decoration of the Prague National Theatre (see p. 112). The most important artist of the 'National Theatre Generation' was the prolific **Mikoláš Aleš**, who did drawings and decorative designs as well as historical canvases. Two examples can be seen here: *The Meeting of George of Poděbrady with Matthias Corvinus* (1877) and *At the Grave of a Fighter of the Lord* (1877), a bleak snow-covered landscape featuring a lone rider on horseback in front of the tomb of one of his comrades.

The turn-of-the-last-century Czech artist best known outside the Czech Republic, **Alfons Mucha** (see p. 108), is represented here only by *Gismonde* (1894), though more of his work can be seen in the decorative arts section. In compensation there is a superb group of paintings by **Jakub Schikaneder**, ranging from beautifully melancholic works such as *All Souls Say* (1888) and *Sorrowful Homecoming* (1886) to the large, suggestive and almost monochromatic *Evening Interior* (1909–10) and *Embankment* (1916–18).

An almost Scandinavian degree of introspection is evident in the penumbral landscapes of **Antonín Hudeček**, which feature the small lake at Okoř (20 kilometres northwest of Prague), where the artist Julius Mařák had a small art school: especially haunting is the work entitled *Evening Silence* (1900), in which a woman with her back to the spectator stares down towards the fading light of the distant lake.

Another lake, the imaginary Black Lake, is an obsessive motif in the works of Hudeček's contemporary **Jan Preisler**, an artist of strong Symbolist orientation whose paintings betray the influence of Puvis de Chavannes and Gauguin. The third outstanding painter of this generation was **Antonín Slavíček**, who created landscapes and cityscapes of extraordinary emotional intensity and pictorial expressiveness, including a number of rain-swept views of Prague and its surroundings.

Troja Château

OPEN	Tues–Sun, 9 am–6 pm, April–Oct; and Sat–Sun, 10 am–5 pm, Nov–March.
CHARGES	120/60 Kč
TELEPHONE	283 851 614
WEB	www.citygalleryprague.cz
MAIN ENTRANCE	U Trojského zámku 1
METRO	nádraží Holešovice, then bus 112
DISABLED ACCESS	Yes
SHOP	Catalogues and guides are available for purchase.

HIGHLIGHTS
Frescoes by Abraham Godyn
Jakub Schikaneder's *Murder in the House* and *An Alley Under Snow*

The magnificent Troja Château, built in 1679–85 for Count Šternberg, was brashly restored in the late 1980s and early 1990s, then suffered extensive flood damage in 2002 when its beautiful grounds were completely submerged in water (luckily the house itself escaped intact).

The rooms on the upper floor boast one of the most extensive cycles of Baroque frescoes to be seen in the Czech Republic, including, in the side rooms, some amusing allegorical ceiling paintings and illusionistic landscapes on the walls. The enormous *Grand Hall* is covered all over with magnificent frescoes by Abraham Godyn set in an ambitious cartoon-like framework featuring fictive architecture and tapestries, one of which shows a Moor plunging head forwards into the room.

The building's principal *façade* is its southern one, dominated by a monumental double-staircase profusely decorated with statues of gods and goddesses battling with Titans. It overlooks one of the earliest examples in Bohemia of a French formal garden, the terraces of which, sloping down to the river, are adorned with eccentric ornamental vases.

Troja Château

Ten of the château's rooms are now open to visitors and contain a collection of 19th-C Czech paintings belonging to the Prague City Gallery. Many of the leading Czech artists of this period are represented, though largely with minor works; the arrangement is roughly chronological.

Among the artists on show are **Josef Navrátil** (*Waiting for the Otter*, c. 1850, *Room 1*), who painted gouache landscapes as well as still-lifes of extraordinary freshness and realism; **Josef Mánes** (*Forest Motif*, 1853, *Room 2*), whose extensive travels through the Silesian and Moravian countryside inspired him to paint scenes of traditional rural life and folk culture; **Adolf Kosárek** (*Red Rocks in the Alps*, 1857, *Room 3*), who drew much inspiration from the special atmosphere of Alpine regions; and **Julius Mařák** (*Pasturing at Dusk*, c 1880, *Room 3*), an artist famous for his romantic woodland scenes.

The leading representatives of Czech Realism include the Courbet-inspired portraitist and still-life painter **Karel Purkyně** (*Room 5*); the landscapist and genre painter **Soběslav Pinkas** (*Room 5*); and **Viktor Barvitius** (*Room 5*), who rejected history painting in the 1860s and turned to the portrayal of city life in Paris and Prague.

The fin de siècle is represented here by **Mikoláš Aleš** (*A Hussite on the Baltic shore*, *Room 6*), who depicted scenes from Bohemian history and folk-tales; **Adolf Liebscher** (*An Excursion to Říp*, 1878, *Room 6*), whose sentimental idylls were inspired by the Pre-Raphaelite Edward Burne-Jones; and **František Ženíšek** (*Room 6*), a painter of historical scenes and allegories. But the highlight of the collection is undoubtedly a group of eerily atmospheric city scenes by **Jakub Schikaneder** (*Room 6*), including *An Alley Under Snow* (1907–1909) and the terrifying *Murder in the House* (1890), in which the suggestive mood is often enhanced by twilight and mist.

in the area

National Technical Museum (Národní technické muzeum) Kostelní 42. Open Tues–Sun, 9 am–5 pm. 220 399 111. This surprisingly good museum has sections devoted to astronomy, horology, photography and telecommunications, but the highlight is the enormous Hall of Transport, crammed to capacity with every conceivable form of transport from the early 19th C onwards. The exhibits are arranged in three galleries around the hall and also in the centre of the room, where old biplanes and even a hot-air balloon hover above a traffic jam of old cars and trains (including the luxury train carriage in which Emperor Francis Joseph travelled in 1891). *M* to Vltavská **Map p. 128, 3D**

Prague Exhibition Ground (Výstaviště Praha) Dukelských hrdinů. Open Tues–Fri, 2 pm–9 pm; Sat–Sun, 10 am–9 pm. 220 103 111. The main site of the 1891 Jubilee Exhibition. The focal point is the Industrial Palace (Průmyslový palác), a large glass and ironwork structure that served as the Exhibition's main hall. Near the palace is a pavilion containing a vast panorama by Luděk Marold of the *Battle of Lipany of 1434*; the canvas is displayed in a darkened setting, surrounded by earth, sticks and other objects, the whole forming a powerful illusionistic recreation of the battlefield. *M* to nádraží Holešovice **Map p. 128, 3-4B**

Lapidarium of the National Museum (Lapidárium Národního muzea) Výstaviště 422. Open Tues–Fri, 12 pm–6 pm; Sat–Sun, 10 am–12.30 pm and 1 pm–6 pm. 233 375 636. Situated within the Prague Exhibition Ground (see above), this remarkable museum features many of the originals of famous public statues and monuments in Prague that have been replaced in situ by copies. Examples include the bronze statue of *St George and the Dragon* from the courtyard of Prague Castle and the 14th-C tympanum from the north portal of the Týn Church on the Old Town Square. The museum also has countless other Czech sculptures from the 11th–19th centuries, the majority in storage because of insufficient space. *M* to nádraží Holešovice **Map p. 128, 4C**

commercial galleries

Galerie Display Bubenská 3, 604 722 562, www.display.cz. Open Wed–Sun, 3 pm–6 pm. Founded in 2001 inside a former recovery centre for alcoholics, this ambitious and fiercely independent new gallery has already made a big name for itself on the alternative art scene. Its aim is to showcase the work of unknown Czech artists and foster dialogue between local and international art communities. Besides regular three-week exhibitions, it also runs film and video screenings, performances, lectures and presentations. *M* to Vltavská **Off map p. 128**

 eat

AT THE MUSEUMS

€ **Trade Fair Palace** Dukelských hrdinů 47. This rather spartan restaurant beyond the main foyer offers snacks and a small selection of main courses. Nothing special, but convenient if hunger pangs strike. There is also a bright and spacious, if rather sterile, Internet café, with windows onto the street. It is situated before the gallery's cash desks and therefore open to non-patrons as well. *M* to Vltavská **Map p. 128, 4C**

SURROUNDING AREA

€ **La Crêperie** Janovského 4. 220 878 040. This enticing French crêperie is just around the corner from the Trade Fair Palace and is a much better place to eat than the museum's own restaurant. *M* Vltavská **Map p. 128, 4D**

€€ **Brasserie Ullman** Letenské sady 341, 233 378 200. On the ground floor of a manor house (Letenský zámeček) in the Letna Park, the Ullman serves an imaginative combination of Czech and French cuisine at reasonable prices. The popular beer garden in front of the house has wonderful river views. *M* Vltavská **Map p. 128, 3D**

€€€ Belcredi Letenské sady 341, 233 375 604. This upmarket French restaurant is located on the first floor of the Letenský zámeček, just above Brasserie Ullmann (see above). *M* to Vltavská **Map p. 128, 3D**

Hanavský pavilon Letenské sady 173, 233 323 641. Good-to-variable Czech cuisine is here combined with live piano music and breathtaking views of the city. Most impressive is the building itself, an exuberantly eclectic structure built for Prague's Jubilee Exhibition of 1891 that mingles the neo-Baroque with tentative Art Nouveau forms. *M* to Malostranská **Map p. 128, 1D**

shop

FOOD

Délicatesse Kostelní 16, 220 571 775. This tiny French bakery is the place to get tasty pastries, salads, sandwiches, quiches and croissants. The shop also does a cheap and reliable delivery service within Prague, if you happen to need it. *M* to Vltavská **Off map p. 128**

VIVA – Potraviny pro zdraví Kamenická 21, 0723216990. VIVA is one of very few shops in Prague catering to vegetarians. Come here for your organic and macrobiotic dry goods, as well as teas, oils and organic soaps. There is also a good greengrocer's next door. Helpful service. *M* to Vltavská **Off map p. 128**

WINE AND BEER

Pivní Galerie U Průhonu 9, 266 712 763. A beer-lovers paradise—this 'beer gallery' has 30 types of Bohemian, Moravian and Slovak beer, which you can sample in the tasting room before you buy. *M* to nádraží Holešovice **Off map p. 128**

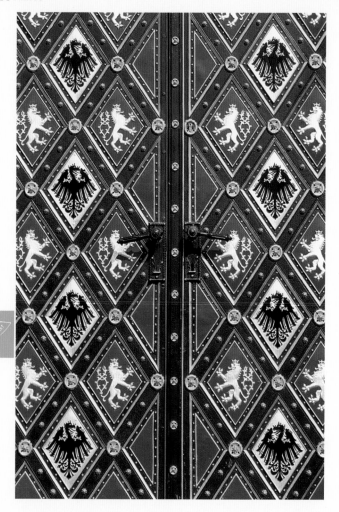

entertainment

INFORMATION
TICKETS
OPERA & CLASSICAL
JAZZ
THEATRE & DANCE
CINEMA
DANCE CLUBS
BARS & PUBS

INFORMATION

The best place to find out about cultural events in Prague is the PIS (see p. 171), whose offices are dotted around the city. A useful source of listings information is the **Prague Post** (www.praguepost.cz), published weekly, which has news and reviews of films, plays, exhibitions and concerts. The monthly **Prague In Your Pocket** (www.inyourpocket.com), available from selected newsstands, is another good source of up-to-date information. For articles on culture, entertainment, politics and life in the city, look out for the glossy quarterly **Prague**, available for free at many tourist offices and travel agencies.

TICKETS

Tickets for cultural events can be bought through one of the city's specialised ticket agencies. **Ticket Pro** has a good online booking service (www.ticketpro.cz) and call centre (296 329 999) as well as outlets at Václavské náměstí 38 (open Mon–Fri, 9.30 am–6 pm; Map p. 9, 2D), Štěpánská 61 (open Mon–Fri, 9 am–5.30 pm; Map p. 104, 3C) and inside the offices of the PIS (see p. 171).

    Bohemia Ticket International (www.ticketsbti.cz) has outlets at Na příkopě 16 (open Mon–Fri, 10 am–7 pm; Sat, 10 am–5 pm; Sun, 10 am–3 pm; 224 215 031; Map p. 9, 2C) and Malé náměstí 13 (open Mon–Fri, 9 am– 5 pm; Sat, 9 am–1 pm, 224 227 832; Map p. 8, 4C). Alternatively, you can buy tickets direct from a venue's box office.

Franz Kafka

Several sites in Prague are associated with the writer Franz Kafka, who was born here in 1883. The house at No. 3 Celetná, just off the Old Town Square, was the Kafka family's home between 1896 and 1901, where the writer's street-facing bedroom inspired one of his earliest stories, *The Window onto the Street*. At No. 19 Wenceslas Square, originally the Prague headquarters of the Trieste-based insurance company Assecurazioni Generali, the 24-year-old Kafka began his first job in October 1907; a medical certificate attesting to 'nervousness and cardiac excitability' allowed him to leave the company the following year. Kafka's only fictional work specifically to mention places in Prague was his novella *Description of a Struggle* (1904–05), an hallucinatory account of a journey through a deserted nocturnal city. In other works, notably *The Trial* (1925) and *The Castle* (1926), the setting, though unspecified, can easily be imagined as Prague, with the cathedral referred to as St Vitus Cathedral, and the eponymous castle as the Hradčany. Kafka's grave, marked by a Cubist tombstone, is situated in the New Jewish Cemetery, outside the city centre (*M* to Želivského).

CONCERT VENUES
OPERA & CLASSICAL

Municipal House (Obecní dům) náměstí Republiky 5. 222 002 336, www.obecni-dum.cz. Box office open Mon–Fri, 10 am–6 pm. The splendid Smetana Hall (see p. 108) is one of Prague's most important cultural venues. Each year it hosts the inaugural concert of the Prague Spring Festival (May 12–June 2) and it is also the home of the Prague Symphony Orchestra. The concert hall and the Art Nouveau Municipal House itself can by visited by guided tour (see p. 106). *M* to náměstí Republiky **Map p. 104, 3B**

Rudolfinum Alšovo nábřeží 12 (náměstí Jana Palacha). 227 059 352 (tickets), www.czechphilharmonic.cz. Box office open Mon–Fri, 10 am–6 pm, and 1 hour before performances. Concerts are held in the beautiful Dvořák Hall. One of the main venues of the annual Prague Spring Festival. The Czech Philharmonic—one of the country's best orchestras—has its base here. Recitals of chamber music take place in the intimate and impressive Suk Hall. The neo-Renaissance Rudolfinum (see p. 39) also has an art galley and on-site café set in a superb columned hall. *M* to Staroměstská **Map p. 8, 2B**

Estates Theatre (Stavovské divadlo) Ovocný trh 1. 224 215 001, 224 901 448 (info about repertoire), 224 901 487 (tickets), www.narodni-divadlo.cz. The main box office (Ovocný trh 6, Kolowrat Palace) is open daily, 10 am–5.30 pm. The on-site box office opens 1 hour before performances. This is the oldest theatre in Prague (1794), set in an elegant neo-Classical building. Mozart's operas *Don Giovanni* and *La Clemenza di Tito* were premiered here. Aside from opera, the building is the main venue for ballet and modern dance productions put on by the National Theatre. Despite major refurbishments, the basic structure of the building has changed little over the past two centuries. The concert scenes for Miloš Forman's *Amadeus* were filmed in the beautiful auditorium. *M* to Můstek or náměstí Republiky **Map p. 9, 1C**

National Theatre (Národní divadlo) Národní 2. 224 901 111, 224 901 448 (info about repertoire), 224 901 487 (tickets), www.narodni-divadlo.cz. The main box office (Ovocný trh 6, Kolowrat Palace) is open daily, 10 am–5.30 pm. The on-site box office opens 1 hour before performances. A beautiful neo-Renaissance building (see p. 112), the main venue for opera, ballet and drama productions put on by the National Theatre. The repertoire concentrates on Czech opera, especially Smetana and Dvořák. *M* to Národní třída **Map p. 104, 1C**

State Opera (Státní opera) Wilsonova 4. 296 117 111, 224 227 266, www.opera.cz. Box office open Mon–Fri, 10 am–5.30; Sat–Sun,

1 pm–5.30 pm; and 1 hour before performances. Established in 1887, the building originally housed the main German theatre in Prague, which merged with the National Theatre after World War II. Since its recent privatisation, the State Opera is now a wholly independent institution. It concentrates on French, German and Italian opera, with performances held in the gilded neo-Rococo auditorium. *M* to Muzeum **Map p. 104, 4C**

Bertramka (Mozart Museum) Mozartova 169. 257 318 461, www.bertramka.cz. Box office and museum open Apr–Oct, Tues–Sun, 9.30 am–6 pm, and Nov–Mar, 9.30 am–5 pm. An 18th-C villa (see p. 96) where Mozart stayed on his many visits to Prague. The chamber music concerts take place Tues–Sat in the garden (summer only) and in the 18th-C salon (other seasons). There are regular performances of works by Mozart and various Czech composers. *M* to Anděl **Map p. 84, 2D**

Vila Amerika (Dvořák Museum) Ke Karlovu 20. 224 923 363. Museum open Tues–Sun, 10 am–5 pm. Concerts at 8 pm, Tues and Fri, summer only; tickets available through Bohemia Ticket International (see above). This jewel-like building is a museum dedicated to the composer Antonín Dvořák (see p. 117). Chamber concerts of Dvořák's music, with the performers dressed in period costume, are held in the intimate upstairs salon. *M* to I.P. Pavlova **Map p. 104, 3D**

JAZZ

U Staré paní Michalska 9. 603 551 680, www.jazzinprague.com. Open daily, 6 pm–2 am; live music Tues–Sat, from 9 pm. Situated in the hotel of the same name, U Staré paní focuses on contemporary jazz played by first-rate local artists. *M* to Národní třída or Můstek **Map p. 8, 4C**

AghaRTA Krakovská 5. 222 211 275, www.agharta.cz. Open daily, 7 pm–12 am; live music Mon–Sun, 9 pm–11 pm. A long-established club that organises Prague's annual jazz festival and manages to pull in a number of top international acts. *M* to Muzeum **Map p. 104, 3C**

Reduta Národní 20. 224 933 487. Open daily, 9 am–3 am; live music Mon–Sun, from 9 pm. Booking advisable; box office open Mon–Fri from 3 pm and Sat–Sun from 7 pm. Prague's oldest and most famous jazz club is very popular among tourists. Its most recent moment of glory was the 1994 visit of President Clinton, who played his saxophone here before a global audience. *M* to Národní třída **Map p. 8, 3D**

U Malého Glena Karmelitská 23. 257 531 717, www.malyglen.cz. Open daily, 10 am–2 am; live music Mon–Sun from 9 pm. Named after its founder Glen Spicker, U Malého Glena has raucous jazz and blues nights in its tiny cellar. The ground floor café offers cheap, American-style food. *M* to Malostranská **Map p. 51, 2C**

THEATRE & DANCE

Archa Theatre (Divadlo Archa) Na Poříčí 26. 221 716 333 (box office), www.archatheatre.cz. Box office open Mon–Fri, 10 am–6 pm and 2 hours before performances. Prague's best avant-garde theatre: music, drama and dance and a variety of top local and international acts. *M* to náměstí Republiky **Map p. 104, 4A**

Theatre on the Balustrade (Divadlo Na Zábradlí) Anenské náměstí 5. 222 868 868 (box office), www.nazabradli.cz. Box office open Mon–Fri, 2 pm–7 pm and 2 hours before performances on Sat and Sun. The theatre rose to prominence in the 1960s when playwrights like Václav Havel established themselves here. Today the repertory continues to focus on serious Czech-language drama, with occasional performances of Havel's plays. *M* to Staroměstská **Map p. 8, 2C**

Black Light Theatre Prague of Jiří Srnec Reduta Národní 20. 224 933 487 (box office), www.blacktheatresrnec.cz. Box office open Mon–Fri from 3 pm; Sat–Sun from 7 pm. When Jiří Srnec created 'Black Light' theatre in 1961, he unwittingly gave rise to a genre that has been pulling in the crowds ever since. This combination of puppetry, mime, music and dance has actors in fluorescent costumes performing against a black backdrop lit by ultraviolet light. No words are spoken, so 'Black Light' can be enjoyed by Czechs and foreigners alike. *M* to Národní třída **Map p. 8, 3D**

Image Theatre (Černé divadlo Image) Pařížska 4. 222 329 191 (box office), www.imagetheatre.cz. Box office open daily 9 am–10 pm; performances daily at 10 pm. 'Black Light' theatre with an emphasis on pantomime and modern dance. *M* to Staroměstská **Map p. 8, 4B**

Magic Lantern (Laterna Magika) Národní 4. 224 931 482 (box office), www.laterna.cz. Box office open Mon–Sat, 10 am–10 pm; performances at Mon–Sat, 10 pm. A famous Prague institution, whose brilliant illusionistic spectacle of stage-sets, actors, music and film premiered at the Brussels World Exhibition in 1958. Though in recent years the show has been knocked off its pedestal by more radical productions in the 'Black Light' mould, this slick multimedia experience still manages to impress. For years housed in the Adria Palace, the Lantern's new home is an extraordinary brutalist building of glass-coated blocks (Nová scéna), situated next to the National Theatre. Booking advisable. *M* to Národní třída **Map p. 104, 1C**

CINEMA

Oko F. Křížka 15. 233 382 606, www.kinooko.cz. Communist-style cinema offering an authentic retro experience, complete with very uncomfortable seating and suspicious staff. Czech and foreign films, up to four each day. *M* to Vltavská **Off map p. 84**

Aero Biskupcova 31. 271 771 349, www.kinoaero.cz. Small but deservedly popular art house cinema showing cult films and old classics, usually original language. There are also frequent retrospectives and theme nights. Good on-site bar. *M* to Želivského **Off map**

Evald Národní 28. 221 105 225, www.evald.cinemart.cz. New Czech films (with English subtitles) as well as documentaries and art house flicks. The small screen is compensated by the comfortable seating and good sound. *M* to Národní třída **Map p. 8, 4D**

Lucerna Vodičkova 36. 224 21 69 72, www.multikino.cz. Watch your movie in style at this fabulously ornate and becomingly shabby Art Nouveau cinema situated in the Lucerna Shopping Arcade. New Hollywood releases are generally screened in English. Lobby bar. *M* to Můstek **Map p. 104, 3C**

MAT Karlovo náměstí 19. 224 91 57 65, www.mat.cz. A film buff's paradise, offering an eclectic mix of mainstream fare, art-house movies, documentaries and old Czech newsreels. The screening room is tiny, so booking is advisable. Most films are subtitled. On-site bar. *M* to Karlovo náměstí **Map p. 104, 2C**

Palace Cinemas—Slovanský dům Na Příkopě 22. 257 181 212, www.palacecinemas.cz. A big brash ten-screen multiplex located in the Slovanský dům shopping centre. Come here for your Hollywood blockbusters and butter-flavour popcorn. *M* to náměstí Republiky **Map p. 104, 3B**

Světozor Vodičkova 41. 224 947 566, www.kinosvetozor.cz. Current releases as well as art-house movies and classics. The Czech films have English subtitles. Two screens. *M* to Můstek **Map p. 104, 3X**

DANCE CLUBS

Solidni nejistota Pštrossova 21. 224 933 086, www.solidninejistota.cz. Open daily, 6 pm–6 am. An unrepentant pick-up joint, complete with cheesy music, expensive drinks at the oval-shaped bar and a mass of lithe gyrating bodies. *M* to Národní třída **Map p. 104, 1C**

Roxy Dlouhá 33. 224 826 296, www.roxy.cz. Open daily, 8 pm–5 am. Rivalling Radost FX as Prague's best dance club, the Roxy is actually a whole complex spread over several floors. The rather tatty interiors host experimental film and theatre, fringe art shows as well as alternative bands and DJ acts. Clubbers chill out next door at Dahab, a Turkish-style tea-room with comfy sofas. *M* to náměstí Republiky **Map p. 9, 1B**

Radost FX Café Bělehradská 120. 603 18 15 00, www.radostfx.cz. Club open 10 pm–6 am; café and lounge open 11 pm–4 am. Glitzy and very cool basement dance club, with local and international guest DJs playing house and funk. The ground floor café serves veggie stomach fillers late into the night. Not to be missed is the groovy lounge at the back, where hardened expats will regale you with stories from the bad old days. *M* to I.P. Pavlova **Map p. 104, 4D**

Karlovy lázně Novotného lávka 1. 222 220 502, www.karlovylazne.cz. Open daily, 9 pm–5 am. A huge multi-level dance club set in a former bath-house by the riverside, complete with a choice of sounds, chill-out rooms, and a basement café with free Internet access. Frequent live bands. *M* to Staroměstská **Map p. 8, 2C**

Lucerna Music Bar Vodičkova 36 (inside the Lucerna Shopping Arcade). 224 277 108, www.musicbar.cz. Bar open daily, 8 pm–3 am. A popular concert venue for local pop, rock and blues bands. Big international acts play at the adjoining Velký sál (Great Hall). *M* to Můstek **Map p. 104, 3C**

Akropolis Kubelíkova 27. 296 330 911, www.palacakropolis.cz. Open 7 pm–4 pm. A good concert venue and smoky basement club, now threatened with closure. Two bars, a chill-out room, and DJs playing unusual music from around the world. With its separate menu for pets, the ground-floor restaurant is definitely the only club in Prague to bring your cat to. *M* to Jiřího z Poděbrad **Off map**

Mecca U průhonu 3. 283 870 522, www.mecca.cz. Open Fri–Sat, 10 pm–6 am. This huge disused factory space in the northern district of Holešovice is one of the hippest dance venues in town. Top DJs, three bars, and even an on-site restaurant. *M* to Vltavská **Off map**

Futurum Zborovská 7. 257 32 85 71. Open daily, 9 am–3 pm. A state-of-the-art dance club and gig venue, converted from a former community centre. Ultra-modern sound and light systems, good DJs and a very popular 80s night (Fridays). *M* to Anděl **Map p. 84, 4D**

N11 Národní 11. 222 075 109, www.n11.cz. Open 4 pm–2 am. A very slick, newly renovated rock club, with live music every night. On-site bar and restaurant. *M* to Národní třída **Map p. 104, 1C**

Czech Beer

Czech beer, generally regarded to be the best in the world, has a reputation going back to the Middle Ages. The general consensus of opinion is that the finest beers are the light and creamy ones from the Bohemian towns of České Budějovice (the original Budweiser or Budvar) and, above all, Plzeň, where the bottom-fermented Urquell or Prazdroj brew served as the prototype for Pils-style beers throughout the world. Prague's own beers (slightly more bitter than the ones above) include Staropramen, Braník and Měštan. The most widely available dark beer is Purkmistr, while slightly treacle-like home brews are served at two of Prague's most tourist-loved beer halls—U Fleků (see p. 161) and U Zlatého tygra (see p. 159). Gambrinus, Radegast and, to a lesser extent, Velkopopovický kozel, are other popular beers found in pubs around the city. With all this quality on offer, and relatively low prices, it is hardly surprising that Czechs are heavy beer drinkers—the average annual per capita consumption is 161 litres, the highest in the world. Pubs usually offer a choice of 10° (desítka) or 12° (dvanáctka) beers, the latter being darker in colour and slightly more alcoholic (up to 5 per cent by volume).

BARS & PUBS
OLD TOWN & THE JEWISH DISTRICT

Bugsy's Pařížská 10 (entrance on Kostečná). Lively upmarket cellar bar with a book-length list of cocktails to choose from. *M* to Staroměstská **Map p. 8, 4B**

Chateau Jakubská 2. A big, noisy and hugely popular bar crammed with drunk students looking for love. *M* to náměstí Republiky **Map p. 9, 1B**

Divinis Wine Bar Týnská 23. This cosy wine bar on a quiet street is a new favourite among local politicians and celebrities. The wine list includes some superb Italian vintages as well as up-and-coming Czech contenders. You can make a dinner out of prosciutto crudo, marinated olives and some Sicilian reds. *M* to Staroměstská **Map p. 9, 1B**

Duende Karoliny Světlé 30. Unobtrusive bar near the riverside populated by an urbane arty crowd. Great place for a quiet one-on-one. *M* to Národní třída **Map p. 8, 2D**

James Joyce Liliová 10. A raucous Irish pub that pulls in the tourists with its all-day breakfasts and decent, if overpriced, Guinness. For a more sedate experience, try U Krále Jiřího next door. *M* to Staroměstská **Map p. 8, 3C**

Konvikt Bartolomějská 11. A small, traditional beer hall, usually crowded with students. Pilsner, Gambrinus and Kozel are on tap, accompanied by a range of snacks—regulars swear by the nakládaný hermelím (camembert stuffed with onion, garlic and chillies). *M* to Národní třída **Map p. 8, 3D**

Marquis de Sade Templová 8. Enormous ground-floor room with a charmingly unkempt Central European feel. Friendly service, cheap drinks and a twenty-something crowd. *M* to náměstí Republiky **Map p. 9, 1B**

Molly Malone's U Obecního dvora 4. Definitely the best and friendliest of the Irish pubs in Prague, set in a charming backstreet location and with endearingly rambling interior. *M* to Staroměstská or náměstí Republiky **Map p. 9, 1A**

Roxy Dlouhá 33. A dilapidated former cinema spread over several floors that hosts occasional live gigs but most of the time serves as a very cool and popular dance club. *M* to náměstí Republiky **Map p. 9, 1B**

Tretter's V kolkovně 3. American-style cocktail bar inhabited by a mix of expats and well-to-do Czechs. Considered pricey by Prague standards, but a top-of-the-range, temple-thumping Mojito will only set you back about €5. Lively weekend atmosphere enhanced by sharp service and 70s soul. The same management runs next door's Ocean Drive, the

place to be if you're a Czech model looking for a rich husband. *M* to Staroměstská **Map p. 8, 4B**

U Medvídků Na Perštýně 7. An unpretentious, authentic Czech beer hall of medieval provenance. Tasty snacks and excellent Budvar on tap. Turn right as you enter the building. *M* to Národní třída **Map p. 8, 3D**

U Vejvodů Jilská 4. A huge, centrally located pub/restaurant serving hearty Czech food and a range of local beers, including the somewhat rare Tmavý ležák. *M* to Staroměstská or Národní třída **Map p. 8, 3D**

U Zlatého tygra Husova 17. A popular former haunt of the writer Bohumil Hrabal, and mentioned in several of his writings. For instance, from *The Magic Flute* (1989): 'And I was at The Golden Tiger, deep in thought, saying to myself, as I always do, that if the Gods loved me I would expire in front of a glass of beer...' The bar has certainly lost some of its earthy charm since the great man's death, and is now an obligatory stop on every tourist itinerary, much to the annoyance of the regulars. Come early if you want a seat. *M* to Staroměstská **Map p. 8, 3C**

HRADČANY
U Černého vola Loretánské náměstí 1. Unlike most Prague pubs, this one closes at 10 pm due to noise regulations in the castle district—a shame, because it is possibly the best pub in the city and one of the few places in Hradčany where local residents can actually afford to drink. Tourists are not unwelcome, but finding a free table is difficult at the best of times. Wait if necessary, because the Velkopopovický kozel they serve here is second-to-none. *M* to Malostranská or Hradčanská **Map p. 50, 3C**

THE LITTLE QUARTER (MALÁ STRANA)
Jo's Bar Malostranské náměstí 7. A travellers' hang-out serving cheap snacks and bottled beer, with a noisy dance floor in the basement. *M* to Malostranská **Map p. 51, 2C**

Na Kampě 15 Na Kampě 15. Situated on the ground floor of a large, recently refurbished building, which also houses the U Karlova Mostu hotel (see p. 177). This lively pub serves decent Czech food and has a beer garden at the back, but unfortunately the river views are obscured by a wall. It is, nonetheless, one of the best watering holes in Malá Strana. *M* to Malostranská **Map p. 51, 3D**

Tato U Sovových mlýnů. A newly opened and (for now) popular student café/bar with adjoining art gallery, scenically located above an old mill in the southern part of Kampa Island. *M* to Malostranská **Map p. 51, 3D**

U Kocoura Nerudova 2. A celebrated pub that had its heyday in the Communist period when frequented by Havel and his friends. Now oriented towards the tourist market, but still worth visiting on account of its excellent Purkmistr beer. *M* to Malostranská **Map p. 51, 2C**

U Schnellů Tomášská 2. One of Prague's oldest and most famous beer haunts, today something of a tourist trap. *M* to Malostranská **Map p. 51, 2C**

U sv. Tomáše Letenská 8. A decidedly tourist-friendly alehouse and restaurant located in the cellars of a former Augustinian friary. *M* to Malostranská **Map p. 51, 3B**

NEW TOWN

Jagr Sports Bar Václavské náměstí 56. If you're attracted by the idea of eating hamburgers and fries while encircled by chrome fittings and TV screens showing American ice hockey, then this is the place for you. *M* to Muzeum **Map p. 104, 3C**

Jazz Café Opatovická 14 (next to the Koruna hotel). Not a live venue and not really a café; rather, just a pleasant bar with eclectic furnishings where you can while away the night hours to some cool jazz sounds. *M* to Národní třída **Map p. 104, 2C**

Novoměstský pivovar Vodičkova 20. Reached from an alleyway off the main street, the 'New Town Brewery' makes its own Novoměstký Kvasnicový Ležák, a fine beer available in light and dark versions. If you're up for it, you can get it in 1-litre mugs and barrel-sized take-away orders. The food menu is meat-based, with steaks, and tasty beef soup with bacon dumplings. *M* to Můstek **Map p. 104, 2C**

Ostroff Střelecký ostrov 336. For an sophisticated experience, look no further than this popular bar on Shooter's Island, where you can sit on stainless-steel chairs sipping exotic cocktails and enjoying superlative views of the floodlit National Theatre. *M* to Národní třída **Map p. 104, 1C**

Pivovarský dům Lipová 15 (corner of Ječná). Another New Town microbrewery. This one makes a range of award-winning beers, which are kept on-site in huge copper vats. The food, advertised outside as 'Czech classics', is nothing more than ordinary pub grub, but the flagship brews certainly justify the journey. *M* to Karlovo náměstí **Map p. 104, 3D**

U Fleků Křemencova 11 Prague's oldest and most renowned beer hall, whose origins date back to 1499. With its frequent cabaret shows and suspect service, the place is now a something of a tourist trap. However, the feisty house brew ('Flek') is still as excellent as it ever was, and you can see how it's made at the on-site Brewery Museum (open Mon–Sat, 10 am– 5pm). *M* to Národní třída **Map p. 104, 2C**

U Kalicha Na Bojišti 12. 'The Chalice' gets considerable mileage out of being mentioned in Jaroslav Hašek's famous book, *The Good Soldier Švejk*. Were it not for this fortuitous literary connection, the management could surely not justify the inflated prices and bland food. However, after a quart (the standard house measure) of Radegast, you might find this temple of Švejkdom somewhat less galling. *M* to I.P. Pavlova **Map p. 104, 3D**

NEAR THE TRADE FAIR PALACE & TROJA CHÂTEAU

Bar Práce Kamenická 9. A tongue-in-cheek shrine to Communism, complete with Socialist Realist portraits of party leaders and assorted memorabilia. Convenient for a well-earned beer after visiting the nearby Trade Fair Palace. *M* to Vltavská **Map p. 128, 3D**

Výletná Letenské sady 32. One of the few pubs in Holešovice that uses an air compressor to store beer—this is the way Pilsner Urquell is meant to be drunk. Now under new management, the pub also offers quick and tasty meals served by friendly staff. *M* to Hradčanská **Map p. 128, 3D**

planning

GETTING THERE
GETTING AROUND
EMERGENCIES & PERSONAL SAFETY
USEFUL INFORMATION
PLACES TO STAY

WHEN TO GO

Prague's climate is typically continental, with warm summers and cold winters, and the best time to visit is either in autumn or spring—with the caveat that spring can sometimes not show at all, but is the most attractive season when it does. Average temperatures in April are between 3° and 12°C (37° and 53°F) and in May between 8° and 17°C (46° and 62°F).

Summer, when the average temperature is between 12° and 23°C (54° and 73°F), sees Prague given over to tourists and very crowded; the air can be humid, with thundery showers. Autumn is a close contender with spring for prettiness, with crisp air, clear skies and an average temperature in September and October between 5° and 17°C (41° and 63°F). Winter is long, cold and grey, and many shops and restaurants are shut, but the romance of Christmas helps break it up. Average winter temperatures are between -4° and +3°C (25° and 37°F).

PASSPORTS & FORMALITIES

Like Poland, Slovakia and Hungary, the Czech Republic joined the EU in May 2004. Visitors from the US, New Zealand, the EU and most other European countries do not need a visa to enter the Czech Republic but do need a passport valid at least six months past the end of the visit. Visas are required of Canadian and Australian citizens, and these must be arranged at a Czech Embassy outside the Czech Republic. For up-to-date information on entry requirements, visit the Czech Ministry of Foreign Affairs' website (www.mzv.cz).

GETTING THERE
BY AIR

Air fares always depend on the season—the high season is the summer and around Christmas and Easter, and weekend flights cost more than those in mid-week.

FROM THE UK

The flight time is approximately two hours.

British Airways www.ba.com, 0870 850 9850 Flies to Prague from London Heathrow at least once a day.

bmibaby www.bmibaby.com, 0870 264 2229. Flights from Cardiff, East Midlands, Manchester and Teesside. Check the website for flight schedule.

Czech Airlines www.czechairlines.com, 0870 444 3747. Departs from London Heathrow, London Stansted, Manchester, Birmingham and Edinburgh.

easyJet www.easyjet.com, 0871 750 0100. Regular flights from Stansted.

flybe www2.flybe.com, bookings 0871 700 0535, general information 0906 209 0005, calls cost £1 a minute. Flights from Southampton.

Jet2 www.jet2.com, 0870 737 8282. Flights from Leeds/Bradford.

FROM THE IRISH REPUBLIC

Czech Airlines www.czechairlines.com, 1 814 4626 operates direct flights from Dublin and Cork to Prague; these tend to be expensive so it may be better to travel via London.

FROM THE USA & CANADA

Czech Airlines (ČSA) www.czechairlines.com, (800) 223 2365. This is the only non-stop carrier from the US, departing from New York. All others make stopovers in Europe. Flights from New York take approximately 9 hours. ČSA also has daily flights from Montreal in the summer, direct to Prague (in Canada call (514) 844 4200).

BY CAR

The drive from the UK to Prague takes at least 18 hours, without an overnight stop. Paris to Prague is 1078 km (670 miles), Brussels to Prague is 925 km (575 miles) and Geneva to Prague is 950 km (590 miles). From Calais/Dunkirk, follow signs to Lille, Brussels, Cologne, Frankfurt and Nuremberg, and enter the Czech Republic at the Waidhaus–Rozadov border crossing. You must have an authorisation sticker (dálniční známka) to drive on any motorway in the Czech Republic. This costs 100 Kč (€3) and is valid for ten days. It is available from petrol stations, post offices and border crossings.

BY TRAIN

Taking the train to Prague only pays if you are under 26 or over 60, as a standard ticket costs more than an cheap airline flight, although unlimited stopovers are allowed. Inter-Rail passes are valid in the Czech Republic and are a good option if you qualify.

GETTING TO THE CITY CENTRE
FROM THE AIRPORT

Prague's airport, **Ruzyně** (220 113 314 for arrival and departure information), was built by BAA and is fairly modern. It is located about 20 kilometres north-west of the city centre, and is only served by buses, although some hotels will collect you if you book ahead.

The **express airport bus** is quick and cheap; it goes to náměstí Republiky and Revoluční every half hour between 8 am and 8 pm. Čedaz, a private company, goes to náměstí Republiky and the Dejvická metro station (the last station on the green line A), and runs every hour from 5 am to 10 pm.

Three **local buses** go from outside the arrivals hall to metro stations every 20 minutes between 5 am and 12 am. No. 179 goes to Metro Nové Butovice (yellow line B); No. 108 goes to Metro Hradčanská (green line A); No. 119 goes to Metro Dejvická (green line A). You can buy tickets from the ticket machines or information desk inside the arrivals hall.

Special **airport taxis** (Airport Cars)—usually white limousines—also operate a service. Normal taxis are not allowed to park at the airport. The airport taxi will cost about €12 (400 Kč) if your hotel is in the centre of Prague, and about €18 (600 Kč) if it is on the far side of town. The company operates a set-price system, so you are not likely to be ripped off.

GETTING AROUND

Prague's public transport system is cheap and efficient, and runs 24 hours every day. The daytime service runs from 5 am to 12 am and the night service from 12 am to 5 pm. Information on the system is obtainable at the information offices of the Prague Public Transport Company (Dopravní podnik hl. m. Prahy)—look for the yellow DP sticker. There are offices at metro stations Muzeum (open daily, 7 am–9 pm) and Můstek (open Mon–Fri, 7 am–6 pm). The staff speak some English and German, and sell travel passes, maps, tram and bus schedules.

TRAVEL PASSES & TICKETS

Travel tickets can be used on any form of public transport—bus, tram and metro. A 15-minute ride above ground (no transfers) or one ride on the metro (no more than four stops) costs 8 Kč. Unlimited travel on all forms of transport, with transfers, for 60 minutes at peak times and 90 minutes off-peak, costs 12 Kč. Children up to the age of 6 travel for free.

Tickets can be bought at PIS offices (see p. 171), newsagents, tobacconists, and anywhere displaying the yellow DP sticker in the window. Tickets can also be bought from the vending machines in metro stations, but these are notoriously complicated to use. Generally, a far better option is to buy a travel pass (časová jízdenka) from one of the DP offices. These cover all forms of public transport and are available for the following periods:

24-hour ticket	70 Kč
3-day ticket (72 hours)	200, Kč
7-day ticket (168 hours)	250 Kč
15-day ticket (360 hours)	280 Kč

A travel pass is valid from the moment you stamp it in a validating machine—you only need to do this once.

Once on board a bus or tram, or before entering the 'paid area' of the metro, you must stamp your ticket in a validating machine. Plainclothes inspectors will make fare dodgers pay an on-the-spot fine and will call the police if you cannot pay. If you pay immediately, the fine is 400 Kč. If you can't pay, you must show your ID and you'll get a bill for 800 Kč.

METRO

The metro is extremely efficient and runs from 5 am to 12 am. Trains are clean and frequent. There are three lines: green line A (Skalka–Dejvická), yellow line B (Černý most–Zličín) and red line C (Ládví–Háje). Further extensions are being planned. There are only three transfer (přestup) stations: Muzeum (where A and C connect), Florenc (where B and C connect) and Můstek (where A and B connect). See the foldout metro map at the end of the book for more information.

TRAMS

Twenty-three tram lines run during the day and eight at night. Trams run every seven minutes at peak times, every 15 minutes off peak, and every 40 minutes at night. Remarkably, they respect—almost to the second—the timetables posted at each tram stop. A good way to see the city is to ride on tram 22, or on 91—the historic tram line. This runs from

Róbert Szabó Benke and Anikó Kuzmich *EUSTRA* (2005)

April to October and takes you on a 40-minute journey from the Prague Exhibition Ground (Výstaviště; see p. 146) through Malá Strana and Wenceslas Square to náměstí Republiky.

BUSES

You will only need to use buses if you are travelling to the suburbs or out of Prague. They run every 10 minutes at peak times, every 20 minutes off-peak, once an hour at night.

TAXIS

To avoid being overcharged, avoid taking taxis near tourist sites and only ever use an authorised taxi. Agree your fare before you get in, or make sure that the meter is on. Ask for a receipt (*paragon*) at the end of your trip. It should have all the details of your journey, including the name of the taxi company and the driver.

The best of way making sure you are not ripped off is to order a taxi by phone. Reputable companies include City Taxi (233 103 310), ProfiTaxi (261 314 151) and Airport Cars (220 113 892).

EMERGENCIES & PERSONAL SAFETY
EMERGENCY NUMBERS

Police 158
Ambulance 155
Fire 150

Street crime has risen dramatically in recent years, but Prague is still a lot safer than many Western cities. Petty crime such as pickpocketing is more likely to affect you than anything more serious. Places to be especially vigilant include the Charles Bridge, Old Town Square, and crowded trams and buses. Be sensible: make photocopies of your passport and note down the numbers of your credit cards. Carry your valuables in a money belt or secure pocket, or leave them in the hotel safe.

Report anything stolen to the police, as you will need documentation for your insurance company. The main police station is at Bartolomějská 6 (open 24 hours). If your passport is stolen, you should also contact your embassy to get a temporary one issued. In case of loss or theft of a credit card, you should immediately stop the card by phoning your bank's emergency number. Visa and Mastercard holders can also call the Komerční banka's emergency number at 224 248 110.

HEALTH & INSURANCE

Britain (but not the US) has a reciprocal agreement with the Czech Republic that entitles British citizens to free medical and dental care in case of accidents or emergencies. The costs of medical insurance can be minimal compared to the potential benefits; when you do receive treatment, do not forget to ask for proof of expenses.

EMERGENCY TREATMENT

Na Homolce Hospital Roentgenova 2. 257 271 111, www.homolka.cz. 24-hour emergency medical care. Most of the doctors speak English and/or German. For dental emergencies, call 224 946 981. **Off map**

Canadian Medical Care Veleslavínská 1. 235 360 133 (724 300 301 after hours), www.cmc.praha.cz. Open Mon, Wed, Fri, 8 am–6 pm; Tues, Thur, 8 am–8 pm. One of the best private clinics in Prague, offering emergency and general healthcare services. **Off map**

PHARMACIES

Pharmacies (*lékárna*) are open until about 6 pm on weekdays. There are 24-hour pharmacies at Belgická 37 (Map p. 104, 4D) and Štefánikova 6 (Map p. 84, 3C). For more pharmacies open around the clock, check the Yellow Pages (*Zlaté stránky*) under *'Lékárny s nepřetržitou pohotovostní službou'*.

EMBASSIES

Canada Muchova 6. 272 101 800. **Map p. 84, 2A**

Irish Republic Tržiště 13. 257 530 061. **Map p. 51, 1C**

UK Thunovská 14. 257 402 111. **Map p. 51, 2B**

US Tržiště 15. 257 530 663. **Map p. 51, 1C**

DISABLED TRAVELLERS

Prague is not the best place for disabled travellers; very few allowances are made for them. Buses and trams are inaccessible for wheelchairs, although trains are a little better, as some have been designed to take wheelchairs, and several metro stations have lifts. For more information, consult organisations in your home country that deal with travel for those with impaired mobility.

USEFUL INFORMATION
MONEY
Credit cards such as Visa, Mastercard and American Express are widely accepted in hotels, restaurants and shops, and there are plenty of ATMs in the city centre and at the airport. Most banks will give cash advances on credit cards, although your credit-card company will probably charge you a fee.

The Czech koruna (crown) is fully convertible. Commission at banks (2%) is less than at the exchange bureaux (up to 6%), but the queues are longer and the opening times less flexible. At the time of writing, 1 Euro was equal to approximately 30 Czech koruna.

PARKING
Parking in Prague can be very difficult. There are lots of resident-only spaces (blue zones), and your car will be clamped or towed away if you ignore regulations (if this happens, call 158). Car theft is not that common, but neither is it advisable to leave your car unattended overnight. Use your hotel's own parking facilities or any car park with 24-hour security, such as the underground 'Centrum' by the riverside opposite the Rudolfinum (see p. 39).

Dining out in Prague
It's a good idea to book a table in the more upmarket places, especially if you visit Prague in the crowded summer months. And in spite of better and more reliable service, it's prudent to scrutinise your bill even at the most established restaurants; creative accounting still persists in Prague. In general, dining hours are early and you may get glares from the staff if you turn up looking for a table after 9.30 pm.

WEB RESOURCES
Central Europe Online (www.einnews.com/centraleurope) Daily news and business information

Welcome to the Czech Republic (www.czech.cz) Information on work, study, travel and business in the Czech Republic

National Rail and Bus Timetables (www.idos.cz) Easy to use and essential if you're travelling out of Prague

INFORMATION OFFICES
The quality of information offices (informační centrum) varies, but most sell brochures, guide books, catalogues, maps and plans. One of the best offices is the **Prague Information Service** (Pražká informační služba), or PIS. Hotel receptions are also a good source of local knowledge. Many visitors buy the **Prague Card**, which includes a transport pass and gives you three days of free entry into over 40 sites around the city as well as free travel on all public transport.

3-day card	€35
7-day card	€37
14-day card	€39

E-Travel Ostrovní 7. 224 990 990-9, www.travel.cz. Open daily 8 am–10 pm. Formerly known as Tom's Travel, this extremely helpful organisation will arrange every aspect of your visit to Prague. The company also has a London office, which can be reached on (020) 7681 2362. **Map p. 104, 1C**

Čedok Na příkopě 18. 224 197 242, www.cedok.cz/ incoming. Open Mon–Fri, 9 am–7 pm; Sat, Sun, 9.30 am–2.30 pm. The former state travel agency, and a good place to buy bus, train and air tickets. **Map p. 9, 2C**

Martin Tour Štěpánská 61 (Lucerna Shopping Arcade). 224 212 473, 224 239 752, www.martintour.cz. Open Mon–Fri, 9 am–4.30 pm. Guided tours for groups and individuals. **Map p. 104, 3C**

Prague Information Service (PIS) Na příkopě 20. www.prague-info.cz Open April–Oct: Mon–Fri, 9 am–7 pm; Sat, Sun, 9 am–5 pm. Open Nov–March: Mon–Fri, 9 am–6 pm; Sat, 9 am–3 pm. **Map p. 9, 2C**

PIS: Old Town Hall (Staroměstská radnice) Open April–Oct: Mon–Fri, 9 am– 7 pm; Sat, Sun, 9 am–6 pm. Open Nov–March: Mon–Fri, 9 am–6 pm; Sat, Sun, 9 am–5 pm. **Map p. 8, 4C**

PIS: Central Railway Station (Hlavní nádraží) Open April–Oct: Mon–Fri 9 am– 7 pm; Sat, Sun 9 am–4 pm. Open Nov–March: Mon–Fri, 9 am–6 pm; Sat, 9 am–3 pm. **Map p. 9, 4D**

TELEPHONE & POSTAL SERVICES
Prague's main post office (pošta) is at Jindřišská 14 and is open from 7 am to 8 pm. Stamps for postcards to the UK cost 6 Kč, to the US 8 Kč. Sending letters to the UK costs 9 Kč and to the US 14 Kč. Mail boxes are orange. Post takes up to five working days to reach the UK, and between seven and ten days to the US.

Most public telephones now run on cards (telefonní karty), which can be bought from post offices, metro stations, kiosks, large department stores, hotels and anywhere displaying a blue-and-yellow Telecom sticker. The cards come with 50 units, 100 units or 150 units.

It can sometimes be a challenge calling AT&T, Sprint and other card companies. If you have problems, call the international operator on 133004. Most operators understand English.

DIALLING CODES

All Prague telephone numbers have nine digits and begin with a 2 (the code for Prague, which must always be dialled, even within the city). The code for the Czech Republic is 420.

To call Prague from the UK: 00 420 + nine-digit number

To call Prague from the US and Canada: 011 420 + nine-digit number

To call Prague from Australia and New Zealand: 0011 420 + nine-digit number

To call Prague from elsewhere in the Czech Republic: 0 + nine-digit number

When calling abroad from Prague, drop the first zero of the local area code. E.g., to call London, dial 00 44 20 followed by the eight-digit number.

INTERNET
Laptops with a modem can use the Quick service (phone 971 103 333; username: quick; password: quick). You will be charged for a local call. Many hotels now provide Internet access, but failing this, you can always check your e-mail at one of the many Internet cafés around the city, such as the Globe Bookstore and Coffeehouse (see p. 121).

OPENING HOURS
Churches, especially famous ones, are often open all day, but sometimes charge an entry fee. Less visited churches may be accessible only during mass or at the visiting times indicated outside.

Museums are open six days a week and are closed on Mondays. They open at around 9 am and close at around 5 pm. Times may vary with the season—museums usually operate shorter hours in winter (Oct–March).

Shops are open Mon–Fri, 8 am or 9 am to 5 pm or 6 pm. Many shops are open until 12 pm or 1 pm on Sat. Some close for lunch and many close in August. Late-night shops are called *večerka*; there are also 24-hour shops called, appropriately, 'non-stop'.

PUBLIC HOLIDAYS
1 January (New Year's Day)

Easter Sunday and Easter Monday

1 May (Labour Day)

8 May (VE Day)

5 July (Cyril and Methodius Day)

6 July (Jan Hus Day)

28 September (St Wenceslas Day)

28 October (Independence Day)

17 November (Velvet Revolution)

24–26 December (Christmas)

TIME

The Czech Republic lies within the Central European time zone (CET). Prague is one hour ahead of the UK and six hours ahead of US Eastern time. The clocks go forward one hour in the summer (usually April/May) and back one hour in the winter (usually September).

TIPPING

At all restaurants, VAT of 22% is included in the price of your food. To tip, round your bill up to the nearest 10 Kč; this may have been done for you already, so check. Don't leave the tip on the table, but pay it with the bill.

PLACES TO STAY

Prague's popularity means hotels should always be booked ahead; rooms are full months in advance for the April to September season. Although hotels tend to charge per room, not per person, some will offer discounts for single occupancy of double rooms, and virtually all will offer discounts to tour groups. If you are staying a while (two weeks, for example) you can get a better deal; in off-season prices fall dramatically, so winter breaks may be an attractive option. For stays longer than a month, you might consider renting an apartment through a lettings agency such as Golgot (Pod stanicí 7, 271 961 582, www.golgot.cz/property).

€ €70–€100
€€ €100–180
€€€ €180 upwards

THE OLD TOWN & JEWISH QUARTER

€ **Penzion Unitas** Bartolomějská 9, 224 221 802, www.unitas.cz. Cheap whitewashed cells with iron doors in a former convent. The building was once used for detainees of the secret police, including Václav Havel (he stayed in the now much-sought-after Room P6). Higher-standard rooms are available on the ground floor and in the nearby Cloister Inn (Konviktská 14), which is run by the same management. *M* to Národní třída **Map p. 8, 3D**

U Krále Jiřího Liliová 10, 222 220 925, www.kinggeorge.cz. A basic bed and breakfast with an excellent location. 12 rooms. *M* to Staroměstská **Map p. 8, 3C**

U Zlatého stromu Karlova 6, 222 220 441, www.zlatystrom.cz. Twenty-one miniscule rooms behind an attractive gabled façade on the 'Royal Route'. There's a disco in the basement. *M* to Staroměstská **Map p. 8, 3C**

€€ **Černý slon** Týnská 1, 222 321 521, www.hotelcernyslon.cz. A UNESCO-listed Gothic building with views of the Týn Church (see p. 15). Recently renovated to a high standard, with a cellar bar and restaurant offering fine Moravian wines. *M* to Staroměstská **Map p. 9, 1B**

Intercontinental náměstí Curieových 43/5, 296 631 111, www.prague.intercontinental.com. Rightly described as a blight on the Prague skyline, and generally packed with tour groups, but with an unsurpassed location at the very centre of the city. Riverside views. *M* to Staroměstská **Map p. 8, 3A**

U Klenotníka Rytířská 3, 224 211 699, www.uklenotnika.cz. Despite the awful décor, this medieval house is unbeatable value for its central location. *M* to Můstek **Map p. 8, 4D**

Ungelt Malá Štupartská 1, 224 828 686, www.ungelt.cz. Medieval building named after the courtyard in which it stands. Ten apartments sleeping up to four people. Booking essential. *M* to náměstí Republiky **Map p. 8, 4B**

U Zlaté studny Karlova 3, 222 220 262, www.uzlatestudny.cz. This impressive Renaissance house situated on the 'Royal Route' retains some original painted wooden ceilings and a 16th-C Gothic cellar. Only four suites and two doubles, so booking is essential. *M* Staroměstská **Map p. 8, 3C**

€€€ **Apostolic Residence** Staroměstské náměstí 25, 221 632 222, www.prague-residence.cz. Charming Baroque building on the Old Town Square, with views of the Astronomical Clock. Only one double room and two apartments, all filled with tasteful antique furniture. Booking essential. *M* to Staroměstská **Map p. 8, 4C**

Casa Marcello Řásnovka 783, 222 310 260, 222 311 230, www.casa-marcello.cz. Atmospheric hotel housed in a building of 13th-C origin once used as a dormitory by the nuns of the adjoining St Agnes Convent. *M* to náměstí Republiky **Map p. 9, 1A**

Four Seasons Veleslavínova 2a, 221 427 000, www.four seasons.com. Luxury modern hotel nestled on the banks of the Vltava River. A combination of three historic buildings, with special

175

suites available in the Baroque section. Impressive views of the Charles Bridge and Prague Castle from the hotel restaurant. *M* to Staroměstská **Map p. 8, 3B**

Josef Rybná 20, 221 700 111, www.hoteljosef.com. Modern hotel designed by London-based architect Eva Jiřičná, winner of an AIA Excellence in Design Award 2003. Bright, airy and minimalist interiors. Most rooms face the summer garden. *M* to náměstí Republiky **Map p. 9, 1B**

Paříž U Obecního domu 1, 222 195 666, www.hotel-pariz.cz. Turn-of-the-last-century elegance reinterpreted for the modern age. Adjacent to Prague's most famous Art Nouveau building—the Municipal House. *M* to náměstí Republiky **Map p. 9, 2B**

U Prince Staroměstské náměstí 29, 224 213 807, www.hotel uprince.cz. A 12th-C building given a complete makeover in 2001. Spacious and beautifully furnished rooms whose ambience is marred only by the noise coming from the square. Seafood restaurant and roof terrace. *M* to Staroměstská **Map p. 8, 4C**

THE LITTLE QUARTER (MALÁ STRANA)

€ **Dům U Velké Boty** Vlašská 30, 257 532 088, 257 534 209, 257 531 360, 257 533 234, www.volweb.cz/rippl. Situated opposite the German Embassy, this discreetly stylish pension is run by a helpful and very friendly couple—Charlotta and Jan Rippl. *M* to Malostranská **Map p. 84, 2B**

€€ **Dientzenhofer** Nosticova 2, 257 311 319, 257 316 830, www.dientzenhofer.cz. Located in the southern half of Malá Strana, this simple and friendly pension was the birthplace of the architect Kilian Ignaz Dientzenhofer (see p. 182). Most rooms have wheelchair access. *M* to Malostranská **Map p. 84, 3B**

The Charles Josefská 1, 257 531 380. Luxury hotel in an elegantly restored 17th-C building, intimate in atmosphere, and with some painted wooden-beam ceilings. *M* to Malostranská **Map p. 84, 3B**

U Červeného Iva Nerudova 41, 257 532 867, www.hotelredlion.com. Gothic, Renaissance and Baroque are all in evidence in this Malá Strana townhouse, the birthplace of the painter Petr Brandl. Several of the rooms have hand-painted wooden ceilings and original period furniture. Convenient for visiting the Castle and its environs. *M* to Malostranská **Map p. 84, 2B**

U Karlova mostu Na Kampě 15, 257 531 430, 257 531 432, www.nakampe15.cz. Converted from a medieval tavern, this large hotel on Kampa Island was reopened in 2003 following extensive flood damage. The ground floor accommodates a lively pub with a beer garden. *M* to Malostranská **Map p. 84, 4B**

€€€ **Best Western** Kampa Všehrdova 16, 257 404 444, www.best western-ce.com/kampa. Located in a quiet street just below Petřín Hill, the Kampa has been recently redecorated in medieval armoury style, complete with swords and shields stuck on the walls and a 'Knight's Hall' restaurant with summer garden. *M* to Malostranská **Map p. 84, 4B**

Pod věží Mostecká 2, 257 532 041, www.podvezi.com. Soberly decorated bedrooms in a wonderfully situated Baroque palace overlooking the Charles Bridge. *M* to Malostranská **Map p. 84, 3B**

U Páva U Lužického semináře 32, 257 533 573, www.romantic hotels.cz/upava. A well-appointed and tastefully restored 17th-C palace in the northern half of Kampa Island. Some of the 27 rooms have outstanding views up to Prague Castle. *M* to Malostranská **Map p. 84, 4B**

U Tří pštrosů Dražického náměstí 12, 257 532 410, www.utripstrosu.cz. Occupies a famous building at the foot of the Charles Bridge. This was once Prague's most endearing hotel; although it is now slightly lacklustre, at least the riverside views remain as enchanting as ever. Rooms have beamed ceilings and antique furnishings. *M* to Malostranská **Map p. 84, 4B**

U Zlaté studně U zlaté studně 4, 257 011 213, www.zlatastudna.cz. A 16th-C house in a fairytale location, with spectacular views over the spires and rooftops of the Little Quarter. From the restaurant you can walk through beautiful terraced gardens all the way up to the Castle. *M* to Malostranská **Map p. 84, 3A**

Waldstein Valdštejnské náměstí 6, 251 556 457. Hidden away in a quiet corner of the square, the Waldstein boasts elegant apartments with original 17th-C painted ceilings situated around a pleasant courtyard. *M* to Malostranská **Map p. 84, 3A**

NEW TOWN (NOVÉ MĚSTO)

€ **Salvator** Truhlářská 10, 222 312 234, www.salvator.cz. Central location close to the Municipal House with simply furnished but clean rooms, some with shared bathrooms, set around an inner courtyard. *M* to náměstí Republiky **Map p. 104, 3B**

U Šuterů Palackého 4, 224 948 235, www.usuteru.cz. Bargain-priced pension set in a fine 18th-C Baroque house with Gothic elements visible in the atmospheric restaurant and some of the rooms. About 100 metres from the metro and Wenceslas Square. *M* to Můstek **Map p. 104, 2C**

€€ **Grand Hotel Evropa** Václavské náměstí 25, 224 215 387, www.evropa hotel.cz. Art Nouveau splendour gone somewhat to seed. This will appeal to those who prefer architecture and atmosphere over comfort and cheerfulness. Frosty service rules at the Evropa, but the price is a bargain for Wenceslas Square, and the famous café and the hotel's Titanic restaurant are not to be missed. *M* to Muzeum **Map p. 104, 3C**

Hotel 16 u sv. Kateřiny Kateřinská 16, 224 920 636, www.hotel16.cz. Small, family-run hotel located close to the University Botanical Gardens. Friendly atmosphere. Some rooms with garden views. *M* to I.P. Pavlova **Map p. 104, 2D**

Nad Zlatém kříži Jungmannovo náměstí 2, 224 219 501, www.goldencross.cz. Spacious if plainly furnished rooms, at a very reasonable price considering the excellent central location. *M* to Národní třída **Map p. 104, 2B**

€€€ **Esplanade** Washingtonova 19, T 224 501 111, www.esplanade.cz. Despite major renovation carried out in recent years, the Esplanade retains the same marbled, chandeliered magnificence of the original 1920s structure. Imposing yet friendly and intimate, this is in many ways the most appealing of Prague's luxury hotels, and is in easy reach of the Central Railway Station. The restaurant serves excellent French food in an Art Nouveau setting. *M* to Hlavní nádraží **Map p. 104, 4C**

Hotel Élite Ostrovní 32, 224 932 250, www.hotelelite.cz. A small modern hotel housed in a 14th-C building with a pleasant open atrium. The popular Ultramarin restaurant offers grilled Mediterranean cuisine on the ground floor, while its basement cocktail bar doubles as a Latin dance club. Top marks for friendly and efficient service. *M* to Národní třída **Map p. 104, 2X**

Palace Panská 12, 224 093 111, www.palacehotel.cz. A grand turn-of-the-last-century establishment fully refurbished in 2000, with first-class service and prices to match. Located approximately 200 metres from Wenceslas Square. *M* to Můstek **Map p. 104, 3B**

Radisson SAS Alcron Štěpánská 40, 222 820 058, www.radissonsas.com/praguecs. A revamped 1930s Art Deco building catering primarily to an international business clientele. Service and facilities of the highest standard are what one would expect from the Radisson chain, and the Alcron does not disappoint. The seafood restaurant was voted 'Best Prague Restaurant' by the Gourmet Dining Guide 2002. *M* to Můstek **Map p. 104, 3C**

art glossary

Aleš, Mikoláš (1852–1913) A central figure of the 'National Theatre Generation' (so-called because virtually all the country's important artists were involved in the construction of the National Theatre and other ambitious buildings in Prague in the last years of the 19th C). Aleš depicted scenes from Bohemian history and folktales, and at the National Theatre (see p. 112) collaborated on a great patriotic cycle entitled *My Country*. His lively and very decorative style was ideally suited to book illustration and after 1882 he virtually abandoned oils to devote himself to graphic art.

Art Nouveau A late-19th-C style that sprang from a revived interest in the decorative arts. It was characterised by elegant sinuous lines and stylised forms derived from nature, such as twisting tree trunks or flowing hair. In architecture, interior design and the applied arts, Art Nouveau used the technical and expressive opportunities offered by the new materials of iron, glass and concrete.

Baroque A style that lasted from the early 17th-C to the mid-18th-C. It was characterised in architecture by grandeur, the use of curved structures and an emphasis on symmetry and illusion, and in painting voluptuous figures, huge landscapes and dramatic subjects. Baroque art and architecture was was used by the Catholic Church as a vehicle to spread its teachings in reaction to the Protestant Reformation.

Brandl, Petr (1668–1735). The leading Czech painter active in Bohemia at the beginning of the 18th-C. Brandl was an artist as varied in his style and subject matter as Karel Škréta—he did heroic French-style portraits, but also dark, religious canvases in which the paint is handled with an agitation reminiscent of the sculptural effects of Matthias Braun.

Braun, Matthias Bernard (1684–1738) One of the most brilliant sculptors of the European Baroque. Born in North Tirol and trained probably in Italy, Braun came to Prague in about 1710. That year he executed for the Charles Bridge (see p. 18) *The Vision of St Luitgard*, a dynamic sculptural group of astonishing technical virtuosity, very painterly in its approach to stone. In later years, his art had an agitated, almost hysterical energy.

Brokoff, Jan (1652–1718) and **Ferdinand Maxmilián** (1688–1731) Like all the other main sculptors of the Bohemian Baroque, Jan Brokoff took part in the decoration of the Charles Bridge (see p. 18) supplying a bronze statue of *St John of Nepomuk*. His son, Ferdinand Maxmilián, began his career collaborating with his father, but soon surpassed him both in technique and imagination, evolving a heavy monumental style enlivened with vivid touches of realism.

Brožík, Václav (1851–1901) A member of the National Theatre Generation (see p. 112) who studied landscape painting in France. He made a name for himself in Bohemia with two large historical canvases—*Master Jan Hus before the Council of Constance* (1883) and *The Election of George of Poděbrady as King of Bohemia* (1898). Many of his less well-known works are on display at the Troja Château (see p. 142).

Classicism A style in art and architecture that was—particularly its late 18th-C manifestation—inspired by Greek and Roman models and characterised by balance, simplicity, harmony, proportion and restraint. Classicism either refers to the art produced in antiquity or to later art inspired by antiquity; Neoclassicism always refers to the latter.

Dientzenhofer, Kilian Ignaz (1689–1751) A native of Bavaria who became the leading Baroque architect in Prague. Dientzenhofer popularised in Bohemia a dynamic architectural style with undulating façades and interiors, plans based on intersecting ovals, a rich play of convex and concave surfaces, piers that project diagonally into the nave, and Gothic-inspired cross-vaulting. The supreme expression of this style is the Church of St Nicholas in Malá Strana (see p. 86).

Fischer von Erlach, Johann Bernhard (1656–1723) An outstanding Viennese architect whose work was essentially Italian in inspiration. Though active mainly in Austria, he executed one of Prague's most magnificent palaces, the Clam-Gallas Palace (see p. 38), which reveals the influence of Palladio while at the same time accommodating dynamic statuary by the Baroque sculptor Matthias Braun.

Gothic The dominant style in European art and architecture between the late 12th and early 16th C. In architecture, the Gothic is characterised by rib vaults, ogival arches and flying buttresses—structural elements which enabled medieval masons to build much taller and larger buildings than their Romanesque predecessors. In painting and sculpture, the Gothic emphasised naturalistic detail and accurate anatomy in figures, but the rules of perspective were not rigorously employed. In the 19th C, the style was internationally revived as neo-Gothic.

Gutfreund, Otto (1889–1927) A member of the pioneering, if short-lived group called Osma ('the Eight'), Bohemia's first avant-garde group of artists, formed in 1907. Gutfreund was a leading exponent of Czech Cubism and perhaps the most outstanding Czech sculptor of the 20th C. After evolving an idiosyncratic Analytical Cubist manner by 1911, later in the decade he moved closer to Synthetic Cubism, before abandoning Cubism altogether after 1920 and producing works in a style that came to be known as Objective Realism. In these last years Gutfreund devoted himself to the realistic but dignified portrayal of the everyday world, which he represented with simple, stately forms, often making use of terracotta; these works were to have an enormous influence on Czech sculptors of the 1920s and 30s.

Kafka, Bohumil (1878–1942) A pupil of Myslbek's, and a sculptor heavily influenced by Rodin, whose Parisian studio he entered in 1904. In later years, Kafka devoted himself to Romantic historical works, culminating in the Jan Žižka Monument in Prague. This enormous bronze equestrian work is one of the city's most famous landmarks.

Kupecký, Jan (1667–1740) A contemporary of Petr Brandl, Kupecký was in many ways the greatest of all Bohemian painters, although he neither studied nor worked in his native Bohemia. An active member of the Moravian Brethren, he was born in Prague but was forced to emigrate with his Protestant parents to western Slovakia before finally settling in Vienna. His friend, the portraitist Johann Caspar Füssli (father of Swiss-born English painter Henry Fuseli), described Kupecký's portraits as combining 'the power of Rubens, the delicacy and spirituality of Van Dyck, the sombreness and magic of Rembrandt'. Another contemporary of his, Anton

183

Graff, wrote that in Kupecký's pictures one found 'true nature, life itself'. The realism of his portraits is certainly remarkable, and it gave much inspiration to Bohemian artists of his time.

Kupka, František (1871–1957) One of the pioneers of abstract painting in Europe, whose work was greatly neglected in Czechoslovakia after World War II. After studying in Prague and Vienna, Kupka settled in Paris in 1895, where he painted a number of vividly coloured Symbolist canvases whilst working principally as a satirical artist and book illustrator. Fascinated by spiritualism and the occult, he developed an interest in the spiritual symbolism of colour, and began experimenting with linear rhythms and colour schemes that he attempted to approximate to the effects of music. After 1909, inspired by high-speed photography, he attempted to portray the effects of movement, and this led in 1912 to the pure abstraction of *Fugue in Two Colours* (now in the Trade Fair Palace; see p. 138). Lyrical abstraction gave way in the 1920s to a more geometric abstract style. In 1923 Kupka published in Prague an influential theoretical work entitled *Creation in Plastic Art (Tvoření v Umění výtvarném)*, and in 1931 was one of the founder members of the France-based Abstraction-Création Group.

Mathey, Jean-Baptiste (c 1630–c 1695) A Burgundian by birth who trained in Rome as a painter but went to Prague in 1675 as architect to the archbishop. The elegance and low relief detailing in his work are very French, and at the Troja Château (see p. 142) he broke away from the block-like or quadrangular Italian villa, introducing a French pavilion system and projecting wings.

Maulbertsch, Franz Anton (1724–1796) Perhaps the greatest 18th-C decorative painter of Central Europe, he specialised in frescoes and altarpieces for churches in Bohemia, Austria and Hungary. His colourful style reveals the influence of Rembrandt and Venetian painters of the period. In Prague, Maulbertsch painted the magnificent ceiling of the Philosophical Hall at the Strahov Monastery (see p. 76)—one of the culminating works of the Bohemian Baroque.

Mannerism A late variety of the Renaissance style in art and architecture, originally developed in Florence and Rome and common in Europe during the 16th C. Mannerism emerged as a reaction to the Classical rationality and balanced harmony of the High Renaissance. It is characterised by the dramatic use of space and light, exaggerated colour, elongation of figures, and distortions of perspective, scale, and proportion.

Mánes, Josef (1820–71) The most accomplished member of a great dynasty of painters, and regarded as the most important Czech painter of the first half of the 19th-C. Mánes was an artist of great versatility, equally adept at portraiture, landscape painting, nudes, Romantic historical works and Classical allegories. His central position in Czech art is also due to his fascination with Slavic folk culture and close involvement with the nationalist revival. He designed banners for patriotic organisations and, in the last years of his life, ensured his lasting popularity by painting delightful scenes of the countryside for the astronomical clock on Prague's Old Town Hall (see p. 11).

Mocker, Josef (1835–99) One of the principal Czech exponents of the neo-Gothic. When Mocker worked, Central European architecture displayed a fantastically over-blown eclecticism that many felt was out of tune with Czech nationalist sentiment. He sought to counter this through restoring and pseudo-Gothic remodelling of 'native' medieval structures, such as the Powder Gate (see p. 35) at the entrance to Prague's Old Town.

Myslbek, Josef Václav (1848–1922) The dominant Bohemian sculptor of the second half of the 19th C, whose richly worked bronzes were admired by Auguste Rodin. In Myslbek's work a romantic Slavonic fervour vies with a strong neo-Renaissance element: in the course of the slow evolution of his St Wenceslas Monument (see p. 115), a wild and romantic portrayal of the saint gave way to a statelier and more sober one. Some of Myslbek's best work is to be seen at Prague's National Theatre (see p. 112).

Parléř, Petr (c. 1330–1399) One of the outstanding architects of the Middle Ages. Parléř probably received most of his training in the Rhineland. In 1353 he was summoned to Prague by Charles IV to work on the Cathedral of St Vitus (see p. 55), where he introduced forward-looking elements like a bold, openwork staircase that would be copied in the cathedrals at Ulm and Strasbourg. His principal contribution, however, was to develop exceptionally inventive and fanciful lierne vaults, curiously similar to English ones built a generation earlier. Perhaps his most enduring achievement was the design of Prague's Charles Bridge (see p. 18), an unparalleled feat of medieval engineering.

Plečnik, Jože (1872–1957) An idiosyncratic Slovenian architect, invited to Prague in 1911 to teach at the School of Decorative Arts. Plečnik later formed a close friendship with President Tomáš Masaryk, who commissioned him to restore Prague Castle (see p. 53) in the 1920s. His greatest work here was the enormous hall (1927–31) between the First and Second Courtyards, featuring a ceiling of copper panels and walls articulated by three superimposed rows of Ionic columns. Plečnik's interest in the architecture of the past, as well as in traditional craftsmanship and materials, made him for many a precursor of Postmodernism.

Reiner, Václav (1689–1743) A prolific artist, one of the chief exponents of illusionistic painting in Bohemia, whose work can be seen in several churches and buildings in Prague. his style was heavily influenced by Padre Pozzo, the most skilful of all perspective experts and quadraturisti.

Renaissance The period in European history immediately following the Middle Ages, marked by a humanistic revival of Classical ideas and values. The Renaissance originated in Florence in the early 15th C, thereafter spreading throughout Europe. Renaissance architecture challenged the elongated Gothic style and emphasis on decoration in favour of a return to Classical proportions and the introduction of perspective. In painting, human subjects began to rival purely religious themes, and naturalism was encouraged by the study of human anatomy.

Ried, Benedikt (c. 1454–1534) An architect of great originality, probably from South Germany, who is credited with bringing the Renaissance to Prague. He was summoned to the city in around 1480 by Vladislav the Jagiellon, and soon superseded all other architects working in Bohemia at the time. As Master of the King's Works, Ried was entrusted with the monumental task of extending the fortifications of Prague Castle and rebuilding the Royal Palace there. For the latter he constructed the magnificent Vladislav Hall (see p. 63)—his chef d'oeuvre—in which

Renaissance features (in the doors and windows) are eccentrically combined with late-Gothic vaulting of a fantasy and complexity virtually unrivalled in the rest of Europe.

Rococo An 18th-C style of art and decoration that originated in Paris as a reaction to the oppressive formality of French Classical Baroque. Its hallmarks were profuse ornamentation, lightness, delicacy and a predilection for asymmetrical natural forms, such as flowers, fruit, leaves, shells and rocks. Rococo painting is dominated by dainty figures and pale colours, and mischievous and frivolous themes.

Romanesque A style in European art and architecture that preceded the Gothic and derived its main impetus from the activity of monastic orders. Typically, churches in this style are low, built of stone, and characterised by round arches, thick walls, small windows and an absence of external decoration.

Šaloun, Ladislav Jan (1880–1946) One of the few early-20th-C Czech sculptors who developed independently of the great Josef Václav Myslbek. Among many fine works, Šaloun made dynamic sculptural groups for the Concert Hall of the Municipal House (see p. 116). But his great achievement was the outstanding Monument to Jan Hus (see p. 14) on Prague's Old Town Square.

Santini-Aichel, Jan Balzej (1677–1723) One of Bohemia's most original Baroque architects, who devised a new style of church architecture, later christened 'Baroque Gothic'. Born in Prague, Santini was the crippled grandson of an immigrant mason from Como. He showed a conventional, if still lively, Baroque manner in his various Prague works, such as the recently restored Ledebour Palace Gardens (see p. 89)—one of several Baroque terraced gardens that give the Little Quarter so much of its charm.

Schikaneder, Jakub (1855–1924) The principal exponent in Bohemia of Post-Impressionism. His highly subtle paintings mark the transition between Czech art of the 19th C and the experimental generation of the early 20th C. Schikaneder began his career painting peasant genre scenes, but ended with haunting and almost abstract evocations of dusk in Prague. His finest works hang in the galleries at the Trade Fair Palace (see p. 130) and Troja Château (see p. 142).

Škréta, Karel (1610–74) A painter of great energy and versatility, though not the genius that is often claimed by Czech art historians. Škréta completed his artistic training in Rome, where he met and painted French painter Nicolas Poussin in 1634. He converted to Catholicism shortly after leaving Italy, and eventually settled in Prague, becoming a prolific painter of altarpieces. As a painter he owes nothing to Poussin, however; he embraces a whole spectrum of Italian Baroque artists from Caravaggio to Guercino and Annibale Carracci. His dark, dramatic canvases sometimes display impressive realism, particularly evident in his portraits, of which the most famous is a lively and informal group portrait of the gem-carver Dionisio Miseroni and his family (now in the Convent of St George at Prague Castle; see p. 67).

Švabinský, Max (1873–1962) Like his near-contemporary Alfons Mucha, Švabinský was a highly successful and versatile artist who worked in many fields, from oil painting and portraiture to the design of stained-glass windows and mosaics. Throughout his life Švabinský's art remained deeply rooted in fin-de-siècle styles. His paintings are strongly Symbolist. He is chiefly remembered today for his exquisite stained glass window of the *Last Judgement* in the Cathedral of St Vitus (see p. 55), and the two long painted panels, containing portraits of leading Czech writers, artists and musicians, which hang in the Municipal House (see p. 116).

Wohlmut, Bonifác (?–1579) A Bohemian court architect whose work is a curious synthesis of Italian and Czech elements. His principal achievement was the upper floor of the so-called Belvedere (see p. 79) in the grounds of Prague Castle. Another important work was the organ loft in St Vitus's Cathedral (see p. 55), which seems at first wholly High Renaissance in character, yet conceals Gothic vaulting behind its Classical arches. Such a synthesis of styles typified the spirit of the Czech Renaissance.

Ženíšek, František (1849–1916) A member of the National Theatre Generation, he produced spirited interpretations of often ridiculous Classical subject matter, involving numerous female nudes. He collaborated with Mikoláš Aleš on the great patriotic cycle entitled *My Country*, and with Václav Brožík and Vojtěch Hynais on the ambitious historical and allegorical murals that decorate the Pantheon of Prague's National Museum (see p. 115).

index

art/shop/eat Prague
First edition 2005

Published by Somerset Kft, a Somerset Books Company
Lövőház utca 39, 1024 Budapest, Hungary
www.blueguides.com
ISBN 963-86727-14

Published in the United States of America by WW Norton & Company, Inc
500 Fifth Avenue, New York, NY 10110, USA

ISBN 0-393-32835-X

A Blue Guides publication

Series devised by Gemma Davies
Editor: Maya Mirsky
Consulting editor: Betsy Maury
Copy and map editing: Mark Griffith
Proof reading (Czech): Zoltán Kálmán

Photo editor: Róbert Szabó Benke
Layout and design: Anikó Kuzmich
Maps by Dimap Bt.
Floorplans by Imre Bába, ©Somerset Kft
Repro studio: Timp Kft.

Felelős kiadó: Ruszin Zsolt, a Somerset Kft. igazgatója

Printed and bound by M.G.I. Print in China.

Front cover: *Seasons 1896* by Alfons Mucha. ©Mucha Trust 2005
Back cover: Photograph by Tomas Vesely

For permission to reproduce pictures throughout the book, grateful thanks are due to the following: The Bridgeman Art Library, London (pp. 23, 72 and 133); the collection of the Jewish Museum in Prague, photographed by Dana Cabanová (p. 31); courtesy of Museum Kampa - Jan and Meda Mladek Foundation (pp. 91, 92); the Prague Jewellery Collection (p. 94); courtesy of the Infant Jesus Monastery (p. 96); ©Mucha Trust 2005 (pp. 109 and 111); TAIZA (p. 123).

Photographs by Zsolt Pataky (pp. 12, 34, 150, 156, 162); Phil Robinson (pp. 14, 58, 88, 99, 113, 117, 131, 143, 148, 172); Jon Smith (pp. 16, 55, 107, 179); Róbert Szabó Benke (pp. 101, 158, 167); Tomas Vesely (p. 10)

SOMERSET BOOKS